ALVIS: The Postwar Cars

ALVIS

The Postwar Cars

John Price Williams

MRP

MOTOR RACING PUBLICATIONS LTD
Unit 6, The Pilton Estate, 46 Pitlake, Croydon CR0 3RY, England

First published 1993

British Library Cataloguing in Publication Data

Williams, John Price
 Alvis: Postwar Cars
 I. Title   II. Blunsden, John
 629.222

ISBN 0-947981-73-X

Typeset by Ryburn Publishing Services; origination
by Ryburn Reprographics, Halifax, West Yorkshire;
colour separations by J Film Process UK, London

Printed in Great Britain by
The Amadeus Press Ltd, Huddersfield, West Yorkshire

Contents

Acknowledgements

Numerous people have helped in the writing of this book, having been persuaded to rack their brains about events of many years ago. I am grateful in particular to Nick Simpson, Technical Editor of the Alvis Owner Club for all his helpful suggestions and for the loan of a great number of pictures from his extensive collection. Another official who was of great assistance was Dave Culshaw, the Club's Registrar, who has an encyclopaedic knowledge of Alvis numbering matters; he has kindly allowed the use of unique pictures of TA 20 chassis development.

Of those who worked at Holyhead Road, Mike Dunn, later of Rolls-Royce, Jack Hedges, Rowland Simmons of Red Triangle, Chris Kingham, Ron Walton and Bill Cassels have provided valuable information; Stuart Peck provided reminiscences of days at Mulliners, Peter Hand of those at Park Ward – later Mulliner Park Ward – and Cliff Petts of Tickford times.

Alex Moulton, Sir David Brown and Harold Beach (ex-Aston Martin) were most helpful on the Issigonis days. Other assistance came from Pam Wearing and M F MacLean of the Rover Group, Bryan Spiers and Don Griffiths of the Association of Healey Owners, Geoffrey Healey himself, Richard Mead the coachbuilder on his days at Dorridge, David Rogerson on those at Duncan and the Rolls-Royce Enthusiasts' Club on Park Ward matters.

A major debt of gratitude is owed to Steve Bagley of the Museum of British Road Transport, Coventry, for his help with my extensive research in the Museum, where much of the Alvis picture material is now stored, and to David Rimmer and Alison Thomas of the Coventry City Record Office which holds the Alvis written archive. Other sources of information have been the Modern Records Centre at Warwick University and the library of the National Motor Museum at Beaulieu, which provided bound volumes acknowledged in the bibliography from which I have taken the liberty of quoting.

The assistance I have been freely given is greatly appreciated.

EASTBOURNE January 1993   JOHN PRICE WILLIAMS

Bibliography

Alvis. *The story of the Red Triangle*. Kenneth Day. (Haynes)
Alvis Gold Portfolio. (Brooklands)
Alex Issigonis. Andrew Nahum. (Design Council)
The Big Healeys. Graham Robson. (MRP)
Cars of the Rootes Group. Graham Robson. (MRP)
Great American Automobiles of the 50s. Langworth/Poole. (Haynes)
Great Marques – MG. Chris Harvey. (Octopus)
Triumph – The Complete Story. Robson/Langworth. (MRP)
The World's Worst Cars. Jacobs. (Bison)
Bound volumes of *Autocar*, *Motor*, *Classic and Sportscar*, *Classic Cars* and *Motor Sport*.

Preface

Alvis is one of the great names of British motoring and yet the name itself has no real meaning. George Lanchester, after selling his own car company and joining Alvis in 1936, used to tell a fanciful story that the firms' directors had wanted to call their cars after a bird, so they chose the Latin word 'avis', but when they realized that this would put them below Austin in alphabetic lists, they added an 'L'.

It was originally the trade mark of a company which made aluminium alloy pistons after the First World War, and more fanciful speculation says that the Alvis is formed from AL, for aluminium, and VIS, the Latin for power. However, the founder of that company, G P H de Freville, disclosed to *The Motor* in 1959 that the facts were very prosaic. When he designed the original Alvis chassis in 1918, he decided to invent a name which would be easy to pronounce in any language: 'From my meditations emerged Alvis and after the name had been settled on, the triangle badge. The word has no ulterior or associated significance or meaning of any kind.'

When de Freville sold the company in 1919 to Thomas George John from Pembroke Dock, in West Wales, they both agreed to continue the name, which became a byword for quality and technical innovation in motoring. Many of the great automobile firms have made little else but cars and trucks, but Alvis in Coventry have always been a first-rate engineering company making, among other things, aero-engines, fighting vehicles and printing machines. However, their reputation is at its most lustrous in motoring.

T G John's first car in 1920 was well ahead of its time with a four-speed gearbox and force-feed engine lubrication. He pioneered front-wheel drive and independent front suspension. The cars of the Twenties and Thirties were almost all highly-engineered sporting carriages; fast touring cars with a reputation for comfort and durability, carrying beautiful handbuilt coachwork by famous names like Vanden Plas, Lancefield, Mayfair, Charlesworth and Cross and Ellis.

Their history has been well-chronicled elsewhere. This is the story of the last quarter-century of Alvis car production; it tells of how and why the company developed its cars after the body-blow of wartime bombing, and of the events leading up to the disappearance from the road of new models bearing the famous red triangle.

There are many classic car owners who like their marque histories to be a recital of unqualified praise for the manufacturer and the models. This Alvis story is one of unfulfilled promise, of disappointment, but also of resourcefulness, ingenuity and pride in a product which is quintessentially British.

(*Author's note*: Readers will notice considerable variation in the quality of the black and white illustrations in this book, especially those which have been reproduced from original factory brochures. In such cases the end result has been much influenced by the method of reproduction and printing chosen for the original brochure, and in other instances by the poor quality of a surviving photograph. I hope readers will understand that the decision to include these illustrations has been taken because of their historical importance – J P W.)

The famous Holyhead Road works which produced all the postwar cars. At the top right are the experimental buildings, where most of the prototypes were built, and at the top left the service department. In between are the foundry and the coppersmiths. The factory was demolished in 1991 and Alvis moved to a new site on the outskirts of Coventry.

The last car produced by Alvis stands outside the Holyhead Road works in Coventry in the autumn of 1967.

A H Raine and Sons' version of the Fourteen, seen here on chassis 21865, was heavily influenced by the Bentley Mark VI.

One of the many variations of 'woody' in the surge of estate car production after the war, which ended as quickly as it began when steel became more readily available and tax advantages disappeared.

Many woodies and utilities met an early end as weather rotted their mainly-wooden bodies. This TA 14, car 22188, has been rakishly rebodied as a four-seater tourer.

The frontal treatment of the TB 14 Sports was an improvement on that of the prototype, but still less than happy.

The TB 14's rear quarters look better than this when the hood has been lowered.

Rowland Simmonds in his 1954 TC 21/100 at speed on the Silverstone loop during the 1982 RAC Rally. Car number 25706 was originally fitted with wire wheels.

Flamboyant Grey Lady 25890, one of the last TC 21/100s, on show at an Alvis Owner Club international day at Duxford. The eagle mascot was never standard on postwar cars, though many owners have fitted them.

This is the car that changed Alvis history and determined the style of the later cars. It is the first fixed-head Three-litre to be bodied by Graber in Switzerland, and was shown on his stand in Geneva in 1953. It was bought from Graber's widow in 1976 by Alvis expert Nick Simpson, who restored it beautifully. It drives extremely well.

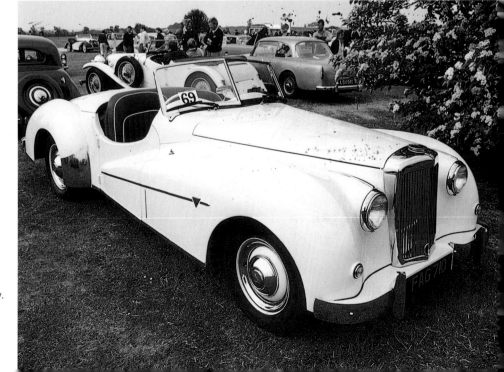

The TB 21, made in very small numbers, was better-looking than its TB 14 predecessor, though much the same from the scuttle back. This lovely example, chassis 25142, was completed in February 1952, but not registered for another year, which suggests sales were slow.

The Willowbrook TC 108/G retained Graber's attractive wraparound rear screen, though this feature was not carried through into the Park Ward cars. This could have been one of the last of the few cars built in Loughborough; it has the highest body number 57013, indicating completion in 1957.

This is how the ill-fated Issigonis Alvis might have looked. These reconstructions are based on line drawings of the car and the recollections of those involved in the project. Typical Issigonis trademarks include the long wheelbase, unstyled frontal treatment and the rather austere interior. Pictures courtesy of *Classic and Sportscar*.

Twin Tickfords with all the Grey Lady trimmings – wire wheels, bonnet scoops and the TC 21/100 legend on the bonnet sides. The hoods can be used in the coupe de ville position.

This Tickford-bodied car, number 25798, was supplied by Brooklands, the London distributor, and was delivered on May 13, 1955 to the titled owner of the West Cumbrian Silk Mills. The flashers are a later safety addition.

Right: The Graber-styled cars always look better on centre-lock wheels, which were not an expensive option. In 1962, when the TD cost just on £3,000, wires were just £34 extra. This left-hand-drive TD Series I has been immaculately restored.

Left: One of the best-known Alvis cars, this is the former works demonstrator and is based on chassis 26741.

One of the early TE 21 convertibles. Hoods were a speciality of the trimming department of Park Ward, who had now become H J Mulliner, Park Ward Ltd. The Everflex hood was offered in six different colours, including this one in blue, and the headlining was in either beige or grey cloth.

14

Nearly half a century separates the 10/30, the first Alvis of the Twenties, and the TE 21, seen together here at the last open day at the Holyhead Road works in August 1989. The 10/30 has the original blue Alvis triangle, which was changed to red and inverted after a legal dispute. 1 ALV, car 27326, is usually on display at the Museum of British Road Transport in Coventry.

Only 105 TF 21s were produced before Alvis car production ceased in 1967. The TF was identical externally to the TE. This 1966 TF, car 27415, has the benefit of a full-length sunroof. Picture from the *Classic and Sportscar* Library.

The noted artist Frank Wootton did a great deal of work for car manufacturers in the Fifties and Sixties before turning to aeronautical subjects and landscapes. He once joked at Alvis that he could produce a better-looking car than Graber at half the price of the Swiss design. Alvis took him up on the challenge. The only stipulations were that there should not be too much overhang at the front and rear and that the curvature of the edge of the roof should have a radius of 3¾ in in case the car was rolled. The project got no further than the drawing board and became another Alvis that might have been. The sculpted door line turned up later in the Volvo P1800.

1

DESTRUCTION
AND REBIRTH

In the afternoon and evening of November 14, 1940, wave after wave of Junkers and Heinkel bombers took off from airfields in Germany heading for the British Midlands. Their aim was to destroy Coventry, the engineering heart of the country. The aircrews' maps had their bombing targets in the city marked with crosses – of which one was squarely drawn over the Alvis car factory on the Holyhead Road. In 12 hours of bombing the Luftwaffe rained down 500 tons of high explosive and 800 tons of incendiaries on the city, causing death and devastation on a scale never before seen in Britain.

The Alvis car factory was almost totally destroyed – but possibly by mistake. The German maps, some of which were seen by Alvis staff after the war, were not up to date. They showed the car factory on the city side of the railway which crosses the A4114, but where their real target stood, the aero-engine works, only open spaces were marked, and this factory was only slightly damaged by comparison.

The low-level raids were prolonged, the explosions huge; typewriters from the car factory were found on the roof of the technical college in the Butts half a mile away. The building burned ferociously. Magnesium which was being used in the manufacture of parts added to the heat, which was so intense that some of the machines melted.

R W Howes, who worked in the finance department and lived nearby, heard that 'the Alvis', as everyone called it, had been hit: 'I went down to the Holyhead Road as far as I could get and it was really ablaze, but I couldn't do anything about it. There were several people standing outside trying to do little bits with buckets and sand, which was hopeless, but they were trying to stop the fire spreading to the houses.'

Howes and two others were first into the ruined factory: 'We found part of Jones the night watchman's leg; that was all there was, with a braid stuck to it.' The next morning, picking through the devastation in the snow and ice, they were machine-gunned by a German fighter. Alvis employees died in this bombing and in a further raid the following April. Although everyone in Coventry knew of the destruction, for security reasons it was not acknowledged publicly until 1945, when Alvis shareholders were officially informed of the 'great and notorious raid'.

It had been the intention of Alvis to continue car production beyond 1939 despite the threat of war, and the 1940 model range included two six-cylinder models, the powerful 4.3-litre and the rakish Speed 25. There was also the 12/70 'big four' 1,842cc model which was to form the basis of postwar recovery. When war broke out in September 1939 car production continued, though at a reduced rate, and in February 1940 the board authorized the production of a further 50 chassis of the 12/70.

T G John, the founder and chairman, had laid out a strategy for the Forties before the war began. This was to produce one chassis with interchangeable engines of 14 and 20hp. The larger six-cylinder would retail at between £500 and £600 and the smaller car at £400. He foresaw production of 3,000 cars per year with Alvis making their own bodies using standard pressed-steel panels. Had the war not put a stop to this, the history and the cars of Alvis would have been very different. As it was, John reported in the spring that the company would continue to supply new cars and service facilities would be fully maintained. He declared ringingly: 'The importance of the car department when happier times arrive is certainly not being overlooked. It is the foundation of our business and it has earned substantial profits.' But November 14, still a few months away, was to change that forecast and Alvis as a car maker would never be the same again.

The saving of Alvis would be the huge demand for armaments now that the 'phoney war' was over. While the car and engine repair departments were dispersed to factories at Stone, Stafford and Leicester, major automotive work quickly came to an end as these dispersal factories and several others started on the manufacture of bomb trolleys, aircraft components and later the overhaul of Rolls-Royce engines from Wellington and Lancaster bombers.

However, the business of producing cars when the war was over was not forgotten. Mulliners, the Birmingham coachbuilders who clothed the prewar 12/70 chassis, had been discussing a razor-edged body of steel panels for Alvis and this was the subject of some elliptical discussion in September 1943 when an Alvis official visited Mulliners. A private letter in the Mulliners archive shows the suspicions Alvis had that Mulliners, who would build bodies for anyone who wanted them, might be working secretly on a more modern design for one of their competitors like Daimler: 'The Alvis man said during our discussion that he had hoped we had nothing else in mind more advanced in body construction as he would not like the body to be behind the times.' However, that option was quickly to disappear, as Louis Antweiler, Mulliners' chief, noted, for the Motor Manufacturers' Society decided later in 1943 that any new postwar bodies could be produced only from existing dies and tools, though this was not a decision which would stick.

This left Alvis at a disadvantage, for during the war the major car makers like Austin, Standard and Morris continued to build cars for the war effort and were given Government money for retooling. Even Humber obtained Government contracts for large cars for officers, and their Pullman, produced directly after the war, was a civilian version of the Thrupp and Maberly staff car. The other luxury car makers, however, were left out, and when in December 1943 Alvis asked the Board of Trade for permission to start work on postwar car development it was refused.

Work, however, did go on to plan for the future – by looking to the past. The car service department, or what was left of it, was by now in an old cardboard box factory at Mount Sorrel, in Leicester, and it was there that the chief designer, William Dunn, drew up his plans.

At the same time, Arthur Varney, a life-long Alvis man who was running some of the factories and was designer of, among other things, the world's first all-synchromesh gearbox, was unofficially redesigning the chassis of the 12/70. He knew several of the outside component makers so well that they made him one-off parts despite the war effort. The car that was to become the TA 14 was put together in a tumbledown hut on waste ground at the rear of the works by two fitters, Fred Lenton and Ivor Cole.

Recalling the prototype many years later, Varney said that they had tried to make it as modern as possible. It was wider and lower than the prewar car, had hydraulic brakes instead of cable, and the 12/70 problem of running on three cylinders instead of four was resolved: 'I thought all this had been done in complete secrecy, but I was inclined to think afterwards that there was no secrecy about it at all, because the weekend we finished it, Captain Smith-Clarke, the General Manager, found it.

'He played Old Harry with me for doing this sort of thing when people were losing their lives in the war.' Varney suspected, however, that Smith-Clarke, who used to prowl around the factory at weekends, had known about the project all along and had waited until it had been finished.

The chassis was first tested using a prewar Speed 25 body, a brand-new unpainted version of which had been found by Varney at the Baginton factory. Charlesworth, the Coventry bodybuilders, mounted it on the chassis where they 'eventually got it going and it was quite a good car'.

One prototype assembled in a shed did not, however, solve the problem of getting ready for postwar production when almost all the facilities had been destroyed and the tooling had disappeared.

As the war came to an end, a crucial decision faced Alvis: should they go into the aero-engine business given their success during the war, should they concentrate on cars, or should they try to produce both? The indications were that big new aero-engine orders were not forthcoming, so the decision was taken to concentrate on cars. Yet there again uncertainty lay, for what car or range of cars should be produced?

An all-important board meeting to discuss strategy took place on February 1, 1945. T G John, by this time a sick man, had recently resigned from the company he had founded a quarter of a century previously. His place as chairman had been taken by A E Nicholson, who was not an engineering visionary and did not seem to have the same sympathy for the car business as other Alvis men.

Nicholson laid out the options. After reviewing the difficulties caused by the Blitz, and the fact that some of their competitors had actually benefited from continuing to produce cars throughout the war, he pointed out the major uncertainties – car tax, petrol tax, purchase tax, possible Government controls and the shortage of materials – which would have a bearing on a new car. Further, no-one could estimate the size or character of the car market in three or four years' time, although he made a guess that the size and power of cars would fall and that prices would also drop 'to extremely low figures'. These last predictions were most important, for Alvis as a luxury car maker would have difficulties surviving in that sort of market. The fact that the predictions were entirely wrong was one of the reasons that restricted Alvis to a basic one-model range for the next two decades.

With minor adaptations to tooling it would have been possible to reintroduce the 3.5-litre six-cylinder Speed 25 from before the war, which had a top speed of nearly 100mph, for the designs were complete, but Nicholson estimated that it would have to be sold at between £1,500 and £2,000: 'No-one', he told the board, 'has suggested to me that more than a few hundred cars at the most could be sold, even on the prewar assumptions as to prices and markets.' It could be reconsidered later if a market appeared and ample money were available to put it on the road at minimum cost.

The Speed 25 had cost £900 in 1940 whereas the 12/70 was less than half the price, at £435. If cars were to be smaller and cheaper it made sense to rework the 12/70, which with some improvements would not be difficult to sell. Indeed, the board was told, the prototype '13.9 car' of the revised version was already running – this being the 'secret' car constructed by Arthur Varney.

The clincher was that the 12/70 had been produced in quite large quantities – more than 700 had been sold – and as the cheapest model, it would test the unknown market without incurring huge costs. The board was reminded that many competitors were well on the way with a postwar car, of which some were thought to be ready to produce brand new models.

The need to proceed was urgent and plans went ahead to build an improved version of the 12/70. In September 1944, the Board of Trade, which controlled all investment and production, had given permission for preparatory work to begin on the prewar car, and a few months later Alvis gave notice that they wanted to spend £35,000 on materials, tools and jigs to make 1,000 new chassis.

Although Arthur Varney's prototype chassis existed as the basis for the revised model, the tooling did not exist for the body. This would have required a major investment, causing a delay in the project. It was a problem solved by an amazing coincidence.

Varney was having a drink one day in the Mill House Hotel at Baginton, in Coventry, when the man next to him asked if Alvis were going back into car production. Varney replied that they were, but although they had a chassis based on the 12/70, all the body tools had been lost in the war. Then, to his considerable surprise, the man told him: 'We're the people who made the body panels for your prewar cars and when they were no longer required they were put at the bottom of the gun-quenching pits at the Royal Ordnance factory on the Foleshill Road – and they're still there!'

These pits, which were up to 100ft deep, were used to dowse naval gun barrels during the manufacturing process. The water was pumped out, and there were the composite steel and wood tools, which were not even very rusty because the water was so still and lacked oxygen. They were then cleaned and altered by Motor Panels of Coventry to give a 4in wider body for the reborn 12/70, now to be known as the Fourteen or, in type-designation, TA 14.

2

THE FOURTEEN – GETTING STARTED

One of the problems which plagued Alvis for the next 20 years was the lack of their own bodybuilding facilities. They had never built bodies and had always relied on outside firms. Although a certain amount of finishing was done at their various premises in Coventry, the Alvis car business was building rolling chassis, finding someone to construct the body and then marketing the finished product.

By April 1945, negotiations to build a body for the postwar car based on the prewar 12/70 had begun with an approach to their close neighbour Carbodies, who nearly half a century on are still in the Holyhead Road making bodies for London taxis. Carbodies estimated that it would take at least a year to put a new saloon body into production. Meanwhile, the experimental car based on the 12/70 was running and another was under construction. Vanden Plas built a model body which was then sent on to Briggs for finishing. Costings were done which brought the price of the new car to £699 plus purchase tax of £195, making a total of £894. Of this, the body cost was to be £160, the dealers' margin would be 20% so that Alvis were left with a profit of only 5%.

In September 1945, Alvis executives and the board members tested the second prototype, which was a lash-up mounted with the Speed 25 body. There was an immediate row since it failed to garner the golden opinions expected by the general manager, Smith-Clarke, and there were calls for more development. At a stormy board meeting he pointed out that the production car would not look like the prototype and demanded that the design be left to him. He opposed any further development, although he did suggest that *The Autocar* and *The Motor* should do secret testing in order for Alvis to iron out perceived problems.

At this stage, he was still planning for there to be a 2-litre 'four' and a 3-litre 'six' on the same chassis, with interchangeable components and independent front suspension. There had already been an experimental car fitted with coil springs and strut-type shock absorbers. The suspension-carrying units were all welded from separate pieces of metal by one of Arthur Varney's fitters as no forgings were available. Though this system was not adopted for the Fourteen it eventually found a place in the Three-litre.

Despite the finish of the war Alvis were still doing aero-engine work, but by the autumn of 1945 they had begun producing components for the new postwar car, which the directors called privately the 'interim' model. There was an official announcement that the new car would be unveiled in the spring of 1946. This optimistic statement was based on a promise from the London coachbuilders Strachans of Acton that they could build 1,000 bodies at £200 each, with delivery beginning in January 1946. The body was specified as being 'like the 12/70, with minor relaxations on quality'.

It is difficult to overestimate the problems of getting the factory back into car production; not only were materials in very short supply, but so much had been lost in terms of tools and jigs. Even drawings had disappeared in the bombing, and worse still, so had duplicate copies of those drawings which had been made for that very eventuality. There was an urgent demand for new parts for the Fourteen and spare parts for the earlier models. Some stock had been salvaged from the bombing, but much had to be completely remanufactured.

Smith-Clarke put advertisements in motoring magazines and newspapers like *The Times*, addressed to Alvis owners, which stated: 'Urgent arrears of spare parts must be provided quickly. Write with information of car number, spares needed ...' The *Coventry Evening Telegraph* reported at the time that as cars were brought into the factory for repairs, parts were dismantled, the components were redrawn with an allowance for wear, and then the drawings were sent to the production areas for the parts to be made as new.

Advertisements had run throughout the war to keep the Alvis name in front of the public, and they had promised 'cars for the connoisseur' once hostilities were over. Now that they were, and a new car had been announced, orders began flowing in. By January 1946, 200 had been received for a car which did not exist, for no bodies had come from Strachans, and worse, it seemed that none were likely to arrive.

By February, there were 300 orders, and the Alvis directors, in panic, ordered Strachans to hand over all the tooling to Mulliners of Birmingham. A deal was done for Mulliners to deliver completed bodies at a cost of between £175 and £200. Alvis would then mount them and fit the front wings.

There were many Mulliners in the coachbuilding business. H J Mulliner, of Brook Street, Mayfair, and Arthur Mulliner, of Northampton, made bespoke bodies. The Mulliners works in Bordesley Green, Birmingham, made a wide variety of bodies for different manufacturers, mainly based on ash frames with steel cladding. The work was spread between two factories, one in Bordesley Green Road and the other in Cherrywood Road, where the Alvis bodies were to be made. Mulliners' range was large; at the 1948 motor show, for example, they displayed bodies for the Armstrong Siddeley Lancaster, Daimler 2.5-litre, Standard Vanguard estate, Lanchester saloon and the Triumph 1800 'razor-edge', which was a development of the body originally designed for the 1940 Alvis Silver Crest, and probably sold-on to Triumph.

They had also made the saloon and drophead body for the 12/70 before the war. This was the first time that Alvis had been involved with what was almost a mass-manufacturing bodybuilder, and the motive was to keep prices down. While the large-engined cars were rakish, fast and splendid, they were also expensive. The 12/70, as already noted, was about half the price and was introduced because of flagging sales of the larger models. It was based on a 1936 Silver Crest design by George Lanchester, who had drawn it after selling his own car company to Daimler. There was also a lineage to a sports saloon body designed by James Wignall of Mulliners on a Bentley 3.5-litre chassis. This was the personal transport of Mulliners' managing director, Louis Antweiler.

The Silver Crest was cheaper to make and sell than other models so there was a feeling, even within the factory, that it was not a proper Alvis. Arthur Varney recalled that one of the difficulties with the car was that its wire-spoked wheels used to collapse while the car was in motion: 'Many people thought that it was a cheap and nasty Alvis motor car.' To a certain extent this reputation also dogged the 12/70, although 748 of the model were sold compared with 520 of the Silver Crests.

What the 12/70 did do was to found the basis for the Fourteen, the most successful single model in sales terms in the firm's history. It was quite similar, but a much better car.

So with Alvis chassis being laid down in the Broad Lane works, which was a wartime factory where engines for Lancaster bombers had been made, and a deal agreed with Mulliners to provide bodies, it seemed that postwar production was about to restart. Mulliners had promised to deliver Fourteen saloon bodies at the rate of 20 per week by mid-June, but ominously the project was already falling behind. By the end of June 1946, only the prototype body had been delivered.

Just as Alvis were dependent upon Mulliners for bodies, so in turn were Mulliners dependent on their suppliers, who were also affected by fuel and material shortages and by labour disputes. Panels for the Fourteen, for instance, came from Forward Radiator at Kings Norton,

Birmingham, which Mulliners later acquired, and from Sankey at Wellington, Airflow Streamlines at Roade, in Northampton, and Carbodies in Coventry. The panels were put on jigs at Cherrywood Road and welded together. Wooden door cappings and facias came from the Awson Motor Carriage Company in Coventry, whose name was the subject of much amusement, but Mulliners made all the wooden framings and upholstery. Indeed, Antweiler made a particular point of concentrating on its quality. There is a story that when he bought a new Rolls-Royce Silver Dawn after the war, he was so horrified by the quality of the upholstery that he had it all taken out and replaced by Mulliners-made leather seating.

Other car manufacturers by this time were well into their stride, which caused Alvis considerable worry. This is evidenced by yet another approach to their neighbour Carbodies. A chassis was delivered across the road to them in January 1947, and a unique aluminium pillarless saloon was constructed on it, which still survives, but Carbodies' view again was that there would be a year's delay before volume production of saloon bodies could start, although they had produced their first drophead by May 1947.

So serious consideration was given to Alvis producing their own bodies at the rate of 15 per week to supplement the Mulliner order and using the same tools and jigs. This was an option which was considered and discarded several times in the following months, although had Alvis decided to proceed with setting up a bodybuilding facility of their own, much future grief and heartache would have been avoided. It would have been perfectly feasible to have done so; their Coventry competitors in Parkside, Armstrong Siddeley, also operating on a fairly small scale, made their own bodies for their brand-new Hurricane and Typhoon, although they contracted-out the Lancaster to Mulliners because of the demand.

While they were still trying to get bodies out of Mulliners to put on the Fourteen, Alvis were already worrying about the bodies for the car which would replace it, and were thinking of moving towards a pressed-steel rather than a coachbuilt body. Regardless of the quality, the saving in cost was huge, but whoever produced it wanted long and large production runs. Briggs put in a quote of £65 per body, but that would have meant ordering 10,000 over three years.

Other diversions that summer were the Government's provision of £160,000 in war damages for the loss of the car factory, the offer from General Motors in America of the Hydramatic automatic gearbox for the new car – it was dismissed as unsuitable by John Parkes, who became chairman and managing director during the postwar period – and an examination of the German DKW, which could have been taken as war reparations. Like Rootes' assessment of the Volkswagen – 'It is too ugly and too noisy ... to build the car commercially would be a completely uneconomic enterprise' – the German car was thought not to be 'our sort of thing'. Smith-Clarke said of the DKW: 'It does not appear to be of outstanding promise ... furthermore there does not appear to be as much interest in Government circles towards the provision of a people's car as some sections of the technical press have suggested.'

Smith-Clarke was probably right about the DKW; it was a fairly crude beast compared with the Volkswagen which, of course, went on to sell well over 20 million.

By now chassis were emerging from Broad Lane at a rate increasing to 20 per week. The first was delivered to Belgium to be bodied abroad, but Mulliners had produced only one body by August, presumably because apart from material shortages, the big manufacturers like Standard were winning priority. Parkes had a threatening meeting with Louis Antweiler, who promised to deliver the first production body by the end of August.

There were now 1,100 orders for a car which did not exist, representing part of the huge pent-up demand for cars now that the war was over. Chassis production was cut back to 10 per week, and desperate efforts were made to find ways of putting bodies on them and getting them into the showrooms, for dealers were complaining that they had nothing to offer their customers.

One method was to build drophead coupes as they were less expensive on resources and could be built in small production runs. Carbodies agreed to build 500 at £195 per body, with a minimum order of 500; Tickford were approached to make a higher quality drophead at half this volume. Other chassis went to the builders of specials and estate cars.

By September 1946, 178 chassis had been built and three Mulliner saloon bodies were delivered, the quality of which was adjudged to be 'most unsatisfactory'. The number of orders began to decline, largely due to a 10% increase in the price of the non-existent saloon from £892 to £1,093.

Yet as winter set in, body deliveries crept up to 10 per week and at the works on November 14, 1946, six years to the day since German bombing had destroyed the original car factory, Smith-Clarke and Stanley Horsfield, the sales director, handed the keys of the first three Fourteen saloons to distributors from London, Glasgow and Belfast. A new era was beginning for Alvis.

Almost ready for production. Note the difference in the shape of the rear window compared with the previous picture, also the mechanism at the sides for opening the windscreen; on the production models a winder was provided in the centre of the dash.

3

THE FOURTEEN
IN PRODUCTION

'This', declared *The Autocar* on that same day in November, 'is a car well worth waiting for', as indeed most Alvis customers in Britain had to for some considerable time.

The Fourteen was so called because of its RAC horsepower rating of 13.58 on which motor taxation was based, and while that continued to be its official title it later became known by its factory designation of TA 14.

The Fourteen was a car which compared very favourably with its 12/70 predecessor. The most noticeable change was in the bodywork, which was larger and more comfortable on its modified chassis. By adding space across the centre – a tactic used to good effect by Issigonis when he redesigned the prototype of the Morris Minor – the length and width were increased by 4in. The added dimensions allowed a longer wheelbase and a wider track, so giving a more comfortable ride. Interior width increased from 47 to 51in and there was a bigger boot, with the spare wheel encased on the outside lid. The wheels themselves were discs, rather than the familiar wires on which most Alvises had ridden. The running-boards also disappeared, as had centralized chassis lubrication, which was replaced by a grease gun.

At the rear, the adoption of a hypoid-bevel final drive gave quieter running inside and made it possible to reduce the height of the propeller shaft tunnel and the level of the floor, so footwells were not necessary and recesses in the back of the front seats gave extra legroom.

There were the traditional Alvis accoutrements inside: polished wood on the facia and door cappings, wide leather seats, door pockets, a flush-fitting sunshine roof and a large 18in sprung-spoke steering wheel. The windows had glass louvres for draught-free ventilation and there was an opening windscreen. However, one perverse omission to driver comfort shared with other pre-Sixties products – with the exception of Rover – was that of a heater, which was available only as an extra.

Despite the redesigned chassis, everything underneath was fairly agricultural. The box-section side-members were braced with several substantial cross-members and the whole unit was suspended on semi-elliptic springs which were damped at front and rear by Armstrong double-acting units. This was from a company which had pioneered independent front suspension on the 1933 Crested Eagle and had installed it as standard on all the prewar 'sixes'. The springs were bolted through Silentbloc bushes, except at the rearward end of the front-spring eyes, where metallic bushes were used for stiffness and to obviate problems arising from the tendency of the crankcase breather pipe to deposit its contents in the area.

Steering was achieved by the Marles cam-and-peg system, the column was adjustable for rake and the brakes were the new Girling double-leading shoe type, but were still rod-operated rather than hydraulic.

The engine was little different from that of the 12/70. The bore was increased by 1mm to 74mm and the stroke remained at 110mm. This gave a 50cc capacity increase to 1,892cc and the horsepower rating went up from 13.22 to 13.58. The new dimensions squeezed slightly more power out of the unit, producing 65bhp at 4,000rpm, which for a car weighing nearly 1½ tons was quite respectable. Indeed, the old 12/70 had been no sluggard for its day, recording 77mph on the Brooklands banking before the war.

The power unit itself was a solid piece of engineering, largely derived from the prewar model and Alvis practice. It was, for instance, a factory tradition to cast the cylinder blocks and then leave them outside for a time to weather, which was a process known as 'pickling'. This was thought to prolong engine life by relieving stresses in the metal before machining. The crankshaft ran in three 60mm white-metal bearings, turned by forged steel connecting rods with light-alloy pistons. A triplex roller chain with

The first postwar brochure promised to exemplify individuality 'to an extent hitherto unattained'.

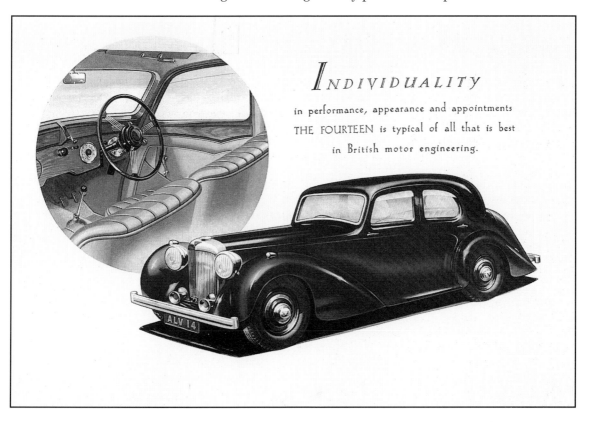

*I*NDIVIDUALITY

in performance, appearance and appointments
THE FOURTEEN is typical of all that is best
in British motor engineering.

THE 'FOURTEEN' ENGINE, a 4 cylinder O.H.V. power unit of just under two litres capacity, notable for its smoothness, silence and outstanding performance.

The 12/70 engine, enlarged by 50cc, gave 65bhp at 4,500rpm, offering respectable rather than outstanding performance.

a spring-loaded automatic tensioner drove the camshaft, operating the overhead valves. The diameter of the inlets was increased to 35mm to give better breathing, being slightly larger than the exhausts.

Fuel was fed from an SU electric pump to a single horizontal 38mm SU carburettor, with a hot-spot of nickel-plated copper between the inlet and exhaust manifolds. The carburettor had a curious device added to it called an After-Burn Eliminator, which, despite sounding like a cure for dyspepsia, was designed to prevent the engine running-on, or 'dieselling' after it had been switched off. This was very common due to timing problems caused by the highly variable octane ratings of 'pool' petrol, which was all that was available after the war. It was a particular problem in the case of the Fourteen, which had a large AC air cleaner in close proximity to the bonnet side. Ron Walton, who worked in the service department at the time, recalled that a bout of running-on would cause the long-stroke engine to thrash about on its rubber mountings, hitting the bonnet loudly and alarming the owner.

The Eliminator worked by closing completely the carburettor butterfly so that no more fuel could enter once the ignition had been switched off. When the ignition was switched on, it opened the throttle enough to allow slow running. It operated by having a special spindle attached to the rear of the ignition switch. Turning the switch then pushed or pulled a Bowden cable, which operated a series of levers and a cam linked to the butterfly. A shortage of supplies meant that some cars were delivered without the device, which led to complaints to the factory.

Another prewar feature was the lack of a dipstick. The oil level was shown by an indicator rod at the side of the engine, which was connected to a float in the aluminium-alloy sump. Those with small garages would have appreciated the adjustable bumper-mounting bars, which could reduce the car's length by 6 inches.

The new car was not without its teething problems. There were complaints about overheating, despite a redesigned cooling system, and many con-rods had to be replaced since the die-casting of the bearings into the big ends led to failure. Piston problems and excessive cylinder wear led to new pistons being tried, and high oil consumption was also common. One senior Alvis employee remembered Smith-Clarke saying that fitting high-quality piston rings was not worthwhile because oil was so cheap! The service department had allowed £15 per car for warranty problems; after the first few hundred cars had been built the cost per car decreased to only £9.

According to his son Mike Dunn, who himself became a chief engineer at Alvis some years later, William Dunn did not like the car, despite being one of the engineers who was involved in the project from the very beginning. The elder Dunn thought that the Fourteen was inferior to the prewar Alvis 12/50, which had pre-dated the 12/70. He particularly objected to the beam axle at the front, which had been dictated by cost.

Nevertheless, the new Fourteen underlined the Alvis reputation for quality and sound engineering in a sporting saloon, and it received a warm welcome. *The Autocar*, in a preliminary test for launch day, called it sure-footed and lively with impeccable all-round refinement. A very high level of excellence, it said, put the Fourteen in the first rank. *The Motor* was able to take it for only a short run, but was impressed by its flexible engine, roadholding and silence. *Motor Sport* paid tribute to 'a rather beautiful unit gearbox', even though there was no synchromesh on first gear.

There were no performance figures since petrol shortages and the climate of austerity dictated against them, but according to Harold Hastings, for many years Midland Editor of *The Motor*, Alvis were most reluctant to offer the car for a full test, even when conditions had improved. He had seen the Fourteen at Holyhead Road and had written in his diary, 'although undoubtedly a very nice motor car, it could just as well have been designed in 1936 as 1946'.

The chassis was wider and longer than the 12/70's, but the springing at the front was fairly primitive, especially since Alvis had pioneered independent front suspension as far back as 1933.

THE "FOURTEEN" CHASSIS

Hastings recalled that *The Motor* had pressed for a test car for three years, but had received no more than vague promises and ingenious excuses. In an article in *Collector's Car* in 1981 he said his suspicions about these excuses had eventually been confirmed: it was because of the improvements in road-testing introduced by *The Motor* after the war, in which all aspects of performance were measured. What had worried Alvis was that on the showing of mere performance figures, the price of the Fourteen might have been difficult to justify. They argued that it was not just what a car did, but the way that it did it that was important; a top speed of up to 75mph or so, a cruising speed of 65mph and flat, predictable handling were quite adequate for the Alvis clientele on the roads of the day. Indeed, those were the kind of figures obtained in a test of the Tickford drophead some years hence, although a later test of a well-used saloon produced 60mph in third gear and only 65mph in top; both tests complained of an over-optimistic speedometer.

In 1947 the Fourteen measured up well against its opponents in terms of both cost and performance and impressed some of the magazines to which it was given for testing, although perhaps less rigorously than *The Motor* would have done. Holyhead Road would have been pleased with the review in the long-defunct *Hutchinson's Motor Magazine* which said excitedly: 'It is lively, unfussy, rippling with muscle ...' They would have been less so with the correspondent of *Country Life* – usually good territory for Alvis owners – who declared rather pompously: 'Generally speaking, the car appealed to me as being better than theory had suggested.'

Alvis were not the only car company producing a warmed-over prewar model. Some of their competitors in the mid-price sporting/luxury saloon market were similarly suffering from shortage of materials and a lack of investment. The Daimler DB18, the Jaguar 1½- and 2½-litre, and the Rover range all had the same Thirties look, with heavy front wings and narrow side windows. There were, however, more modern offerings: the streamlined Armstrong Siddeley, albeit with the prewar 16hp engine, the Riley RM series and the new razor-edge Triumph 1800. There were also, of course, more exotic and expensive sporting cars like the Bristol

400, based on a BMW design, and the Healey Elliott, but possibly one of the closest competitors in terms of price, quality and image was the Lea-Francis Fourteen. It was more sophisticated mechanically, with a twin-cam engine, but Lea-Francis were another specialist Coventry car maker who did not achieve the long-term success they deserved.

Alvis, then, had done their best; they put into production a car of quality and integrity under very difficult circumstances, few of which were of their own making. The car was widely admired as having the traditional Alvis virtues of good looks, solid engineering and fine handling. It harked back in character to the Alvis four-cylinder cars of the Twenties and Thirties, when the advertising of the time used to promote 'fours' as being 'as smooth as a six'. It would be good to relate that Alvis' problems ended with the successful launch of the Fourteen – but unfortunately this was not to be the case.

The first three production cars to come out of the factory after the war are handed over to distributors on November 14, 1946. The sales manager, Stanley Horsfield is on the right.

Export models awaiting shipment to the docks. The Carbodies coupe at the right is destined for Cairo via Alexandria.

4

PROBLEMS AND POSSIBILITIES

The year 1947 was one which most motor manufacturers would have wished to have expunged from the calendar. There was to be one of the coldest winters on record, an acute fuel crisis, massive electricity cuts, a widespread shortage of steel and other raw materials and Government interference in the industry which drove its leaders to distraction.

It started badly for Alvis after a rare occurrence of industrial action. Pattern-makers went on strike because people who had been away from work with long-term illness were dismissed. This meant that they could not benefit from the workers' benevolent fund. Eventually the management withdrew the notices, but not before a mass-meeting expressed strong resentment at the suggestion that the workers were not putting in enough effort.

However, this local difficulty was minor compared with other problems. The Government were now in 'export or die' mode and insisted that the allocation of steel for building cars was to be tied to the number of cars that Alvis and other manufacturers exported. The export quota was originally 30% – against which Alvis achieved 22% – but it then increased to 60% of production, and then again to 75%. The Alvis board were, as they put it, 'in a state of considerable perturbation', for they privately admitted that the Fourteen was not really suitable for export except in certain European markets, many of which were closed anyway due to exchange control restrictions.

British coachbuilt cars had a bad reputation further afield for failing to withstand local conditions: in the tropics the wooden frames distorted and deteriorated because of extremes of temperature and humidity; the Fourteen's springing was particularly unsuited to rough roads, but then neither did it give the 'boulevard ride' to which Americans were accustomed, nor did the Alvis have a six-cylinder engine which the United States demanded in their sedans. Smith-Clarke remarked bitterly on several occasions that if Alvis had realized the export quotas which were to be imposed, they would have designed the car differently, the implication being that they would have gone for a pressed-steel body.

Despite the slim chance, and being desperate to stay in business, Alvis sent their London agent to the United States to investigate the prospects. He returned saying that there could be a market for 100

Alvises a year – if there were a different body. As a result, Duncan Industries in Norfolk, who were already building a special body on the Fourteen chassis, were asked to submit designs for 'continental and touring' models, but apart from the specials which they were already building – detailed in a later chapter – there is no evidence that anything came of the project.

Exports of chassis did begin in 1947 to Belgium and to one market which was to be most significant – Switzerland, where the car was well-received at the Geneva show. Three drophead coupes were exhibited by Swiss builders Worblaufen, Langenthal and Hermann Graber of Berne. Sweden was another market which was being cultivated.

A demonstration chassis went off to South Africa and six more were authorized to follow; hopes were raised of selling 300 chassis and 100 saloons there within a year, but then, mysteriously, the Alvis agent who had promised such sales stopped replying to letters from Coventry.

Progress on production was agonizingly slow: the prototype drophead from Carbodies arrived and was sent back for further modification – a process which took nine more months. A continuous battle ensued with Mulliners over the slow delivery and poor quality of the saloon bodies. Serious faults were reported, and the board of Alvis registered its profound concern at the unsatisfactory state of affairs, which, it said, was having a grave effect on the car business.

The managing director was sent off to bully not only his opposite number at Mulliners, but also one of the firm's other directors. The bodies were supposed to be arriving from Birmingham, fully trimmed, at the rate of 20 per month, but the delays were hardly Mulliners' fault as their works in Birmingham were being shut down continually because of fuel restrictions, as indeed were Alvis.

The disruption of production and increases in the cost of raw materials led to further rises in the price of the chassis and saloon, which were announced as 'an emergency surcharge'. The saloon went up from £1,093, including tax, to £1,225. However, such was the pent-up demand for cars on the home market that the increase had little effect on the order book. In June, for instance, there were more than 150 new orders for the car, although chassis deliveries were beginning to slow down because of the prospect of purchase tax being imposed on the estate car specials.

Evidence of how much the Government tried to control car output and divert as many cars as possible abroad is detailed in a letter to Alvis from the Ministry of Supply. It allowed Alvis to produce only 194 vehicles in the first quarter of 1948, of which a mere 49 would be for the British market. There was a threat that if the export target were not met, the licence for production would then be withdrawn. As it happened Alvis had already delivered more than 49 vehicles to British agents, but decided to keep quiet about it. There was also a great deal of discreet lobbying on behalf of makers like Alvis to reduce the 75% export quota – which they could not hope to meet – and as a result they had their allocation reduced to between 40 and 55%. Even so, Alvis insisted that the Fourteen could achieve only some 20% in exports.

There seems to have been a certain turning of a blind eye to what

was happening. When the Ministry of Supply, for instance, urged car makers to standardize as much as possible on a single car, John Parkes told them blithely that Alvis were 'keenly alive' to such a policy, failing to point out that they were in no position to do anything else. Yet he did extract a concession from them: as the Fourteen was a stop-gap model, he persuaded them of the need to proceed on its successor, which enabled the release of materials to build the prototype.

Smith-Clarke had become irritated with the Government's constant pressure for the export drive and he made a public speech in which he poured scorn on what he called 'the golden road to enormous production', which would be disastrous if it led to the loss of the British tradition of skilled craftsmanship.

However important that tradition, it was still failing to deliver, and by the end of November 1947 saloon bodies were arriving at the rate of only 15 per week. Although Carbodies had begun deliveries of the drophead, they and Mulliners still could not keep up with chassis production, and Alvis considered bringing body supplies more under their control by producing their own pressed-steel channel sections to replace the wooden sections from the bodybuilders.

By this time, Alvis had begun to move slowly away from the idea that cars were to be the main postwar business, and were producing the highly successful Leonides radial aero-engine which was to be used widely in helicopters and fixed-wing aircraft. In addition, they began manufacturing printing machinery. Stories circulated – largely due to the lack of cars – that they were cutting back on car production, which they had to deny in statements to the press, pointing out that the order book was fuller than at any time in the company's history.

Yet there was gloom in the boardroom, for Parkes and Stanley Horsfield had come back from the Brussels motor show at the start of 1948 to report that despite enthusiasm for the Alvis sports TB 14 special there was a problem selling the saloon: 'It was evident, even by cutting our price to the limit, that we could not compete with other British cars in our class.' The need for a new car – still nearly two years away – was urgent.

By the time of the motor show in autumn at Earls Court the home motor industry had orders for 600,000 cars and was producing 300,000 a year, of which 75% were supposedly destined for export. The Fourteen on the Alvis stand was one of the 270 cars at the show, almost all marked 'exclusively for export'.

Despite the problems and pessimism at Holyhead Road, 1948 was the most successful year that Alvis had ever had in terms of vehicle production, turning out 1,143 chassis with saloon, sports and drophead bodies.

The Fourteen was nearing the end of its life and would have gone in 1949 if the Three-litre had been ready. Smith-Clarke had an ambitious plan to build another 1,000 to fill the gap until the new car arrived, but fortunately this was defeated and only another 200 were built. The Carbodies order for drophead coupes was reduced from 500 to 400 as there was some difficulty in shifting them, despite a summer sales campaign.

At the Brussels motor show in 1949, Alvis exhibited the Fourteen as usual – and did not receive a single order. Stanley Horsfield maintained that the sellers' market in Britain and the rest of Europe was beginning to collapse as the postwar demand was beginning to be satisfied, though this seems to have been more an apology for the car than a statement rooted in fact. As the Earls Court show approached rumour spread that a new Alvis was on the way, and only 24 orders were received in September. Deliveries that month were down to 15: eight saloons, five dropheads and two tourers.

The final mechanical modifications were made for the 1950 model year. There were minor changes to the chassis frame, better oil seals in the back axle, which was sometimes fitted retrospectively with the 4.3:1 unit from the TB 14, more grease nipples on the kingpins and an alteration in the brake pedal to give better foot clearance.

The Fourteen was phased out as pre-production work increased on its Three-litre successor. The remaining 95 tourers and 74 saloons were scheduled for completion by June 1950, making a total production run of 3,310 chassis. Of these, only about half carried Mulliners saloon bodies. The final order to Mulliners in June 1949 was for 280 saloons, bringing the total to 1,780. However, Dave Culshaw, the Registrar of the Alvis Owner Club, notes that Mulliners numbers on the bulkheads of the Fourteens run from M1 to M1775, which suggests that fewer might have been made, though it could well be that given the quality problems not all the bodies were accepted by Alvis. A small quantity were built in knocked-down form by Mulliners, but it is not clear what numbering system, if any, was adopted.

The Carbodies quotient made up 400 – reduced from the original order of 500 – and another 100 were accounted for by the TB 14 tourer. The rest of the chassis were bodied by everyone from Tickford to the local carpenter, making the Fourteen the biggest seller of the postwar years and the second most successful single model in Alvis history after the 12/50 of the Twenties and early Thirties.

Many British coachbuilders bodied Fourteen chassis because Mulliners could not keep up with production rates. This is a neat example by Airflow Streamline, of Roade, in Northamptonshire.

5

DROPHEADS AND SPECIALS

The epitome of British coachbuilding has always been the drophead coupe, which is a true test of craft and skill in designing a car to look as good in open form as in closed. This is achieved by making the bodyshell rigid enough to avoid flexing without adding excess weight, and devising arrangements to stow the hood easily and efficiently.

Since only some 1,500 out of 3,000 Fourteens bore Mulliners' saloon bodies, a similar quantity was left to be bodied as estates, specials and of course drophead coupes, which formed by far the greatest proportion. Two Fourteen dropheads were listed by Alvis and both had two doors. The Carbodies version was manufactured in Coventry on the other side of the Holyhead Road, and the Tickford was made by the firm of the same name at Newport Pagnell, in Buckinghamshire.

The Carbodies coupe was regarded as the standard model and retailed in 1948 for £1,275 including purchase tax, which was the same price as the saloon. It had a substantial amount of metalwork in its structure, unlike the Tickford, which employed the traditional method of light-alloy panelling on ash frames. The Tickford was much more expensive at £1,850, and was regarded as being a luxury version. It could be distinguished externally from the Carbodies coupe by the pram irons either side, which tightened the rear half of the hood to enable easy fastening of the peak rail to the top of the screen.

Special features included chrome-plated window frames and Connolly leather-panelled upholstery edged by piping, and a great deal of attention was paid to the hood, which could be erected in three positions. 'Special tailoring' of the hood material was said to prevent wind flap; this meant that the double thickness of material was stuffed with horsehair. Along the two edges of the hood at the sides ran spring-tensioned wires to maintain the shape and rigidity of the material. This is a technique still used by Aston Martin, who eventually took over the firm.

The Carbodies coupe was built down to a price whereas the Tickford Fourteen was a traditional high-quality coachbuilt car, and the first to be bodied by Tickford when they resumed production after the war. Cliff Petts, who worked for the firm for more than 50 years, remembered them bringing a Carbodies coupe into the works to compare the quality with their own. There was a considerable difference in finish; for instance, Tickford would use chrome-plating on capping plates where Carbodies employed aluminium.

The bare chassis arrived at Newport Pagnell having been driven down the A5 from Coventry with the front wings and radiator in place, and the rear wings lashed to the rear of the frame to be mounted on the new bodywork. Effectively, the body was built from the scuttle back, the body and door frames being made up in wooden jigs to ensure uniformity. Each car took some three weeks

The first body produced by Tickford after the war was this Fourteen. It is pictured outside the company's works in Newport Pagnell, to which bare chassis were driven down the A5 from Coventry.

Richard Mead, of Dorridge, in the West Midlands, had a small coachbuilding firm which bodied several makes, including Bristol. This was his first Alvis, chassis number 20566. Note the full-depth doors.

Another Mead-built car featuring Tickford-type pram irons.

A neat special by Jarvis of Wimbledon, on chassis 21421, at Holyhead Road. The Humber in the background was an Alvis factory car.

to build, and the buyers often came to the works to drive away their new and expensive possessions. Since they were paying a third as much again as they would have done for the Carbodies coupe, they were entitled to be spoiled.

Although no factory records now exist, Cliff Petts, Tickford's unofficial historian, estimates that some 75 Fourteen chassis were bodied at Newport Pagnell. Later, considerably more were built on the Three-litre chassis.

The two factory-listed coupes formed only a part of the output of dropheads on the Fourteen chassis. The Alvis export drive had sent chassis to several parts of Europe, where coupes were constructed by notable coachbuilders such as Pennock of The Hague, Vercruysse of Brussels and, as noted, in Switzerland by Worblaufen, Langenthal and Graber.

In Britain small numbers were constructed by Raines, Knibbs in

Richard Mead also used a job lot of prewar MG bodies on Alvis chassis. This decayed car, (chassis number 20626), has sills similar to those of the later Three-litre.

Manchester and Richard Mead at Dorridge, in the West Midlands. Mr Mead, who was still working on Alvises in 1992, having moved to Northern Ireland, was able to give a fascinating insight into the way that freelance coachbuilders worked at the time, constructing aluminium alloy panelling on wooden frames and using anything which they could get their hands on to stay in business when materials were so short.

He produced six Alvis coupes, although only three were to his own design. The others were bodies originally built by Tickford for the MG WA, which was a luxurious 2,561cc version of the SA saloon and went into production in 1938. When MG resumed manufacture after the war with the TC model the surplus WA bodies were advertised as a job lot. 'They were in a barn at the back of a pub in Newport Pagnell. I bought one, and took an option on the others,' he told me. 'I took it back to the Midlands and put it on a Fourteen chassis – and it fitted exactly!'

Some of the bodies in the barn were half-complete, some were panelled, some had doors; in all they made 12 dropheads. Mead put some on other makers' chassis, including one on an eight-litre Bentley, although the rear had to be widened to fit on the chassis. The Mead-designed cars can be distinguished from the ex-MG bodies by the moulding line along the waist of the cars. The Mead cars have a thin line which disappears above the wheelarch; the MG bodies have a much wider band which sweeps down to join the arch. The door shapes are also different.

The way that Mead worked was to advertise his coachworks in *The Autocar*. An Alvis agent would ask for a coupe to be built, deliver the chassis by rail to the station next door to his works, pay a deposit, and then wait up to three months for delivery. For despite a staff of 10, with the exception of the Tickford bodies, almost everything – panelling, upholstery, facia, interior trim and hood – had to be made by hand. The wooden formers for the wheelarches, rear bow section and front screen pillars were made in one piece and then, to ensure a perfect match, were cut down the middle in the sawmill next door, where Mead's father was making laminated sections for the new razor-edge Triumph. The seat frames were handmade in West Bromwich and the hide for the seats came from a dealer in Redditch.

Then there was the Government. In those days of shortages there was, among other restrictions, a Cotton Permit. Any material used for hoods and trim had to be reported to the Customs and Excise. According to Mead, 'They made life unbearable, always breathing down your neck, particularly before a Budget.'

Despite these laborious processes, beautiful bodies emerged, and the Alvises were easier to work on compared with the Bristols and the Jowetts which Mead also bodied. This was because the Alvis chassis arrived not just with an engine on a frame as with the other makes, but was complete with front wings and bonnet in place. Tied to the frame were other components – bumpers, instruments, wiring loom, the rear number box and tools. 'Alvis were always very good at supplying the bits,' said Mead, 'unlike Jowett, who were a joke; their chassis used to arrive without even the electrics.'

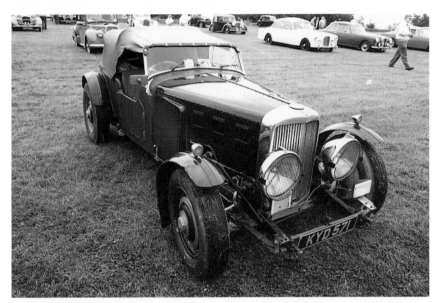

During the Sixties, many Fourteens had fallen into disrepair and were sought-after by specials builders. Some enthusiastic efforts were better than others ...

6

WOODIES AND UTILITIES

To make the most of production rates, Alvis were prepared to sell not only complete cars but also rolling Fourteen chassis with wings at £640, on which no tax was payable. This enabled small coachbuilders to produce their own versions of the Fourteen by combining high-quality Alvis engineering with bodies that they designed and built themselves.

Apart from the major builders like Mulliners, there was still a thriving cottage industry in coachbuilding in the Forties, although this was eventually to cease as more and more manufacturers adopted monocoque chassis, thus depriving the small specialists of a platform upon which to build their sometimes quixotic creations.

Particularly popular in the Forties were the shooting brakes or 'woodies' constructed, as the name implied, of wood, which was plentiful rather than steel, which was not. In addition, there were utilities, or 'utes' as they were known in Australia, which used alloy panels rather than wood.

The reason for the sudden interest in these creations, apart from the steel shortage, was a tax dodge; a utility which was restricted to 30mph was not liable for purchase tax and could qualify as a commercial vehicle, much as owners of Mini-vans avoided the tax in the Sixties. In addition, vehicles with flat floors, which could be used for load-carrying, had almost unlimited access to 'red' petrol, supposedly for commercial purposes, while private motorists were finding petrol severely rationed.

In 1947, hybrid Alvises were being built enthusiastically all over the country. Castle Motor Bodies of Kenilworth, for instance, offered a £1,080 version, with chassis at £640 and body at £440. This actually worked out at £145 cheaper than the Fourteen saloon, which was in short supply anyway because of the problems at Mulliners. Riverlee Motor Bodies of Tyseley, Birmingham, sold one 'retaining saloon car lines' with aluminium roof and side panels; it had only two front seats and a long flat loading floor and it looked rather like a hearse. In the West End of London, the main Alvis distributors, Brooklands of Bond Street, claimed that deliveries of their £1,278 folding rear seat version, which had an opening tailgate rather than rear doors, were 'reasonable'. In nearby Berkeley Square, Kevill-Davies and March were selling a Fourteen with wood above the waist and a fabric roof.

While some woodies had the timber frames on the outside, others were cleverly constructed with internal framing. One such example which still survives, made by Angel bodies of Manchester, has a splendid wood-lath roof exposed inside the car.

Other notable builders of estates were Hector Dobbs of Southampton, who bodied Alvis, Riley and Healey chassis, and car distributors with their own bodybuilding facilities like Caffyns in Eastbourne and Mann Egerton.

Though some manufacturers made scores of bodies, others managed only a few. Lindley of Long Eaton, in Derbyshire, for instance, produced only two woodies, of which one survives, and Richard Mead at Dorridge made only one utility.

To qualify for the Alvis 12-months mechanical warranty the vehicles had to be returned to the works for testing. Ron Walton, then an apprentice in the Service Department, had the job of

An estate by Caffyns of Eastbourne, bearing Eastbourne CBC trade plates. It was probably taken behind their coachbuilding works, since demolished, in Seaside.

running them up the Keresley road to see if anything fell off and whether the body and chassis continued to remain in one piece when the brakes were applied. He recalled that while some of the woodies were properly built by coachbuilders, it was obvious that some had been knocked together by carpenters who had never made a body before, and their work sometimes resembled a chicken shed on wheels. However, such was the postwar demand for new vehicles that anything sold.

It is doubtful whether these strange devices did the Alvis name much good. Indeed, the reputation for high quality probably suffered from some of the more obvious bodging. Yet the chassis surplus had to be used up, and there seems to have been no attempt by the factory to design and contract out a woody or utility version of their own.

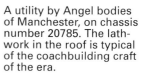

A utility by Angel bodies of Manchester, on chassis number 20785. The lathwork in the roof is typical of the coachbuilding craft of the era.

The boom was shortlived, ceasing as more steel became available for saloon bodies and tax concessions ended. Few woodies have survived because of hard commercial lives and the ravages of weather on wood and fabric. Today, out of 600 Alvis versions made, only about a dozen are thought to remain.

7

TB 14 – SLEEK AND SPORTY

It was not often that an Alvis created a sensation at a motor show, but it certainly did at Brussels and London in 1948 when the company displayed a dramatic streamlined open two-seater, whose swooping lines brought crowds to the stands and, according to the *London Evening Standard*, 'stole a great deal of the limelight' at Earls Court. Certainly ostentatious, even vulgar, it was a great departure from what Alvis had made before, even though the Earls Court brochure called it 'a thoroughbred in the true Alvis tradition, a striking combination of graceful line and quiet, effortless sports performance'.

The car, which became known as the TB 14, had a curious history. It was developed by a Belgian industrialist, Pierre Goldschmid, as a special. The standard 14 chassis was given an extra SU carburettor to push power up from 65bhp to 70bhp and was clad in a lightweight body by F J Bidee. Goldschmid was well-known as a racing driver, and on the car's first outing in competition, at the Grand Prix des Frontieres at Chimay in 1947, it was entered in the 2-litre class and averaged 106km/h (66.25mph). Goldschmid went on to set a Belgian national record of 95mph.

At this stage the car was called the Anglo-Belge, and it was exhibited to some excitement at the Brussels motor show in February 1948, as was another Alvis 14 special, a two-door four-seater coupe by Carrosserie Franco-Belge.

Alvis took up the Bidee design, but made it less 'tank-like' in shape – an echo of the Bugattis of the Twenties. The resultant TB 14 was the last-minute surprise of the 1948 Earls Court motor show, and one of 270 cars to be displayed at the first postwar British show, where most were marked 'for export only'.

The startling crimson bodywork was set off by ivory leather upholstery, but what caught the imagination of the national press in those austere days were two extras: a 'beauty parlour' in the facia, holding a mirror, lipstick and perfume, and a cocktail cabinet built into one of the doors. However, not everyone approved: 'Cars and cocktails are words that come together much too easily and want to be kept a long way apart,' said the *Daily Mirror* censoriously, at a time when drinking and driving was not a major issue. They need not have worried, since the cabinet – two decanters, glasses and a mirrored shelf – did not make it into any of the production cars.

It was the first sportscar that Alvis had offered for nearly 10 years,

A heavily touched-up picture of the intrepid Pierre Goldschmid in his Alvis special, the basis for the TB 14. It set a Belgian record of approximately 95mph.

since the war had put an end to the production of the Speed 25, and it could not have looked more different from the classic roadster of the Thirties.

The front grille, resembling a clover leaf and sometimes unkindly called a mud-splat, flowed downwards much like an Allard's and had the headlamps behind it much like a Peugeot. Sidelights were fixed into the deep front bumpers at the place most likely to be hit. These bumpers were 'particularly massive in order to meet continental conditions', said *The Motor* mysteriously, as if such things were necessary to brush aside foreign hordes.

Other notable features, apart from the flowing bodywork, were a louvred bonnet, a fold-flat windscreen and a 'one-man' hood which could be hinged down and stowed away behind the front seat squab. The price was nominally £1,275, which was exactly the same as the saloon and the factory version of the drophead coupe, although as one of the motoring magazines admitted, it was 'ungettable' and there were only two at the most in existence. Although the appearance was futuristic, the same prewar solid beam axle and semi-elliptic springing mechanicals lay beneath.

Alvis were pleasantly surprised by the attention that this outré creation attracted, and needing a push on the export side, decided in January 1949 to order 100 production versions with coachwork by King and Taylor of Godalming, in Surrey. Six months later little had happened and, finally, King and Taylor admitted that they could not fulfil the contract.

Anxious not to abandon the project, Alvis approached several other coachbuilders – Richard Mead at Dorridge remembers being one of them – but either facilities were not available or the price was too high. The chassis cost of £640 and additional body cost could not amount to more than £1,000 or the dreaded double purchase tax would have come into effect.

By the summer of 1949, the situation was becoming desperate as Alvis wanted to display the car at the autumn Earls Court show. The board was told that something would have to be done quickly because of the 'loss of prestige which was likely to result from not

It caused a sensation at the 1948 motor show at Earls Court, but the styling was to be made more restrained for the production version of the TB 14.

The built-in 'beauty parlour' and cocktail bar also disappeared from the 100 TB 14s which were to be built.

showing a model which had been widely publicized'.

Finally, after much dithering, a contract was signed with AP Metalcraft of Coventry for 100 bodies, with an initial price of £342 each for the first 10; Alvis hoped for a reduction in subsequent deliveries, but Metalcraft refused to drop the price. The body series numbers began at APM 1001 and chassis numbers at 23500.

By this time, the car's appearance had changed for the better. The headlights were taken from behind the grille and mounted in the wings, as were the sidelights; this was presumably to meet the new United States legislation on the height of lamps, which led to the similar change in the Morris Minor, infuriating its designer, Alec Issigonis. In addition, the TB 14's bumpers were simplified and overriders were added. The bonnet louvres also disappeared. The only mechanical changes were a different crownwheel and pinion, giving overall ratios of 4.33, 5.76, 8.36 and 12.86:1. An *Autocar* used-car test in 1953 gave a performance figure of 0–60mph in 21.2sec and a fuel consumption of 23mpg.

Production figures show that only the initial 100 were made, many being versions exported to the Far East and Australia. It was a curiosity of a car, and those left still draw attention, but it was no competitor as a sportscar for its contemporary, the Jaguar XK 120.

The rakish lines of the TB 14 are seen to their best advantage from the side.

8

DUNCAN COUPES AND DROPHEADS

One of the most notable of the TA 14 specials was the Duncan. It was designed and constructed by Duncan Industries of North Walsham, Norfolk, and was sold initially by the Reliance Garage of Norwich. A daring pillarless two-door coupe with a large glass area and wide-opening doors, hinged at the roof as well as the sides, its svelte appearance contrasted sharply with the traditional TA 14. Nearly all were hardtops, although a couple of dropheads were made.

What was remarkable about the Duncan was that there was a Healey version which looked almost identical. The story behind the building of these cars had its origin in the body problems suffered by both Alvis and Healey in 1947. Both were turning out more chassis than could be bodied either by Mulliners for Alvis or Westland and Elliott for Healey, so they cast around for alternatives.

After the war, Ian Duncan, an aeronautical engineer, had set up shop in an old canning factory in North Walsham to produce his own mini-car, the Duncan Dragonfly, which was to be powered by the 500cc BSA A7 motorcycle engine. However, production start-up costs led him to look for other work, and he began by building bodies on Ford chassis. At a chance meeting in the Steering Wheel Club in London, the racing driver Kay Petre told him that Donald Healey was looking for bodies for his chassis – suffering the same problems as Alvis – and a modified Hillman Minx body was put on Healey's frame which was powered by the Riley 2.4-litre engine.

The Reliance Garage at Norwich were Alvis agents and their sales manager, Stan Boshier, was so impressed with the prototype Healey that he asked Duncan to body a Fourteen chassis. The design was drawn by Duncan's colleague, Frank Hamblin, another refugee from the aircraft industry, who was working with him on the Dragonfly. With a few modifications, the new body was mounted to the chassis.

The construction, with no centre pillar, was similar to the Talbot Ten which Hamblin was running at the time. It also had features in common with the Dragonfly body which he had previously designed, although that was much smaller.

Neither Alvis nor Healey seemed to mind very much that the cars were almost identical. Apart from the engine and chassis, they differed only in the radiator – Alvis using the Fourteen shell – and the line of the Healey front wings was carried forward into the front doors, giving them a characteristic bulge.

Most of Duncan's first staff were engineers, not bodybuilders, so Bert Wall was recruited from Wolseley to productionize the car. The first Alvis was produced in the summer of 1947 and there is some suggestion that the car was registered CVG 119 in Norwich. However, this vehicle has the Alvis single car/chassis/engine number 20998, while there are six known Duncans with earlier car numbers beginning at 20549 – this being a mere 49 from the first production model. Given the Alvis rate of chassis production, if CVG 119 was the first Duncan, the chassis must have been lying around for some time.

Duncan soon moved from North Walsham to a former RAF aerodrome at Havringland, about 15 miles away, in order to have more room for production, the staff now having grown to more than 100.

Ian Duncan was quoted as saying that they were trying to produce coachbuilt bodies in the best British tradition. Individual bodies were prohibitively expensive when built to special order, he said, but laying down a fairly large batch had kept prices down and this had been justified by the number of orders received.

Construction began with a frame of seasoned English ash or German beech put together originally not by Duncan, but by two firms of boatbuilders on the Norfolk Broads, Graham Bunn of Wroxham and Herbert Woods of Potter Heigham. Each frame took three weeks to make on a jig: 62 pieces of wood had to be screwed and glued together with Aerolite 300F, the resin used to hold the wooden Mosquito aircraft together. Four steel reinforcements in the windscreen and door pillars stiffened the structure.

Later, Duncan began their own construction, and contemporary pictures show a busy production line of wooden frames at the aerodrome site. However, they did not put on the panelling at that stage. Instead, the frames were sent all the way to the Midlands, where Motor Panels at Coventry clad the frames with high-tensile aluminium alloy panelling and then sent them back to Norfolk to be mounted on Alvis chassis which had come from Coventry in the first place. They were then sprayed and trimmed locally and tested in runs around the airfield.

Extensive soundproofing was used and wood cappings were supplied in acacia or walnut. Other refinements included what were described as 'universally-adjustable' front seats of Dunlopillo trimmed with PVC and offered in green, brown or beige and the customer could choose the exterior colour. The steering column was adjustable for rake, and there was provision for a Clayton heater and an Ekco radio. On the drophead version the head folded almost flush and was hidden by a cover.

The firm's brochure said proudly: 'The combination of the Duncan body and the Alvis chassis provides standards of silence and performance which can only be obtained normally in much larger cars.'

Such handbuilt luxury and style did not come cheaply; in July 1947, the standard Fourteen cost £998 plus £227 purchase tax, a total of £1,225. The Duncan was far more expensive; because the basic price of the car was over £1,000 it was penalized with double purchase tax, coming out at £1,413 plus £792, making a total of

The first Duncan, finished in bright yellow, pictured outside Duncan's works in Norfolk before the first sales trip to Scotland. The pillarless construction is seen here to good advantage.

£2,205. In other words, one new TA 14 and two new Morris Eights could be bought for the cost of a Duncan – with change left over. The Healey was even more expensive at £2,876.

At these prices neither was ever going to be a commercial success, despite the hopes of Ian Duncan. By the summer of 1948 the firm had gone into receivership with the main creditor, HM Customs and Excise for unpaid purchase tax, estimated at about £60,000. One reason might have been that Duncan were also producing the so-called 'spiv cars', which were very basic vehicles without lights, much like kit cars, which escaped the tax.

It is difficult to track down precise production figures, but the Alvis Owner Club think that 30 Alvis-Duncans were built, of which about 15 survive. Ian Duncan, who many years later ran a photographic business at Bletchley, was quoted as saying that he built 70. The Association of Healey Owners believe that some 39 saloons, three coupes and eight two-seaters were built on the Healey chassis. There was also one built on the Daimler 2.5-litre chassis, and in September 1947 the *Daily Sketch* reported that the same Duncan body was to be used for all three cars, which prompted a large row with Daimler, who denied all knowledge of the deal.

It is a pity that the Duncan Alvis was not more successful; when it was launched it drew crowds wherever it stopped and today it is still a good-looking car with a spirited performance, being 2.5cwt (280lb) lighter than the Mulliners saloon. Many were registered in Scotland thanks to a selling trip made in the first car – a dramatic yellow vehicle – by the Duncan works manager David Rogerson, and to the enthusiasm of the Alvis distributor in Glasgow, James Galt.

The Motor World, in a Scottish road test, reported in December 1947 that it was 'a delightful car, one eminently desirable for self-possession' and paid tribute to its impeccable road behaviour. Other notable points were the wide expanse of glass and the 'tasteful furnishings ... which will please even the most fastidious'.

When production of the Alvis and Healey models stopped, Duncan himself sold the prototype of the Dragonfly to Austin for many thousands of pounds and went to work at Longbridge, but Austin had no time for a front-wheel drive, rubber-suspension mini-car. In common with the deplorable practice at Alvis and in almost all the British motor industry at the time, the prototype was broken up. It is a small coincidence that Alec Issigonis, who designed the very same unit some years later, also has a part to play in the Alvis story with a futuristic prototype which met a similar fate.

One of the 15 or so Duncans which survive. It sold for nearly twice the price of the TA14, due to high build costs and penal taxation.

9

PLANNING THE THREE-LITRE

Two months after the first Fourteens had begun leaving the production line in November 1946, Alvis started to consider a replacement, although the Fourteen was to be in production for another four years. John Parkes, now chairman and general manager, decreed from the outset that it should be a three-litre car powered by a six-cylinder engine and that it should be so designed as to be attractive in export markets because, of course, supplies of steel were being linked to car makers' export performances.

This entailed, among other things, development of the independent front suspension which had been used in experimental form on a Silver Crest with airdraulic struts and on a Speed 25 with coil springs.

William Dunn took over responsibility for the design and development of the new car with the title of Assistant Chief Engineer (Cars). The engine was designed by Chris Kingham, who had joined Alvis in 1946 and had spent some time investigating the use of cast iron for crankshafts rather than the forged steel which Alvis had used until then.

In February 1947 the go-ahead was given for the Three-litre prototypes. There were to be three cars, to cost between £5,000 and £6,000 each. The design was done at Alvis by Harry Barber. A clay model was ordered and a year later the Alvis directors inspected the first mock-up. The car, which looked very different from the Fourteen, had a smooth, sculpted look and bore a remarkable resemblance to the Jaguar Mark VII which was to come in 1951. It had a pressed-steel shell with headlights faired into the front wings, whose lines swept through the passenger doors to the rear wheelarch. There was a one-piece bonnet and a divided windscreen with a chrome surround. It looked decidedly modern in comparison with the prewar Fourteen design.

However, the familiar problem appeared again: who was to build the body? In the spring of 1947 negotiations began with Briggs Motor Bodies, a volume producer eventually taken over by Ford, who could make the basic shell for the remarkable price of £65, though the tooling costs they required from Alvis amounted to £200,000. As the talking progressed, the tooling price came down to £150,000, but the basic unassembled shell in primer went up to £95 and the whole body, assembled, painted and trimmed was quoted at £200, with production to begin in 18 months from the time that the

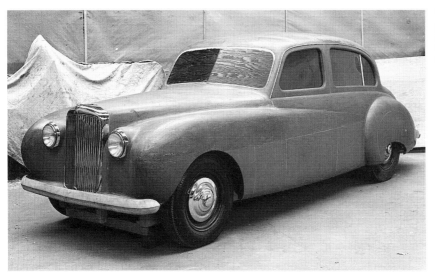

order was placed. There were two drawbacks: Briggs, being in the volume business, wanted to produce 100 shells per week, which was much in excess of the rate at which Alvis could either make chassis, or sell completed cars.

The other fundamental problem, however, was the tooling cost: where was £150,000 to come from when the company's profits for 1947 were to be only £19,000? If money were borrowed to invest in the project, the payback could come only from high volume, to which Parkes was opposed, or high cost. Alvis tried to seek a solution from the Pressed Steel Company itself, but again the tooling costs were huge at £200,000, besides which, no deliveries of bodies could be made until March 1949.

Despite this, development work on the engine and chassis continued and there was even optimistic talk of displaying the prototype at the next Earls Court show in 1948, but this idea was rejected in case it affected sales of the Fourteen. It could only have been shown as a prototype since, although the saloon shell was now on the chassis, it was not driveable.

Negotiations began with Borg-Warner about fitting an automatic gearbox with column control to be manufactured under licence by Alvis, though an Alvis design was also going ahead.

By the end of 1948, one of the experimental six-cylinder engines had completed 100 hours of bench testing. The car had still not been driven, but Parkes assured the anxious Alvis directors who demanded 'exhaustive tests' that it was coming along well and would have a much greater export appeal than the Fourteen. He also told them that his staff were trying to see if they could make it as cheaply as the Fourteen, which was now beginning to show a respectable profit.

In January 1949, the first road tests of the prototype took place which uncovered vibration and steering problems, although these were resolved. It seems likely that the testing was done on a TA 14 vehicle which still exists, chassis/engine number 3L3, with the chassis adapted at the front to carry the new independent suspension, a longer bonnet to accommodate the bigger engine and

The first prototype body undergoing road-testing. The car bore a resemblance to the Jaguar Mark VII, which was to appear some years later in 1952.

Rear-end treatment was rather fussy, but in general the car had elegant lines and would have been a worthy bearer of the Alvis badge.

a Speed 25 radiator. As it looked much like the Fourteen, testing of the new engine could be done in some secrecy.

Another prototype, which carried the new saloon bodywork, was numbered 3L1 and ran on factory trade plates 092 WK. The car was then registered in Coventry as HWK 768 on February 15, 1949. Parkes, who believed in hands-on management, took one of the prototypes for a 260-mile run. He described it as 'very satisfactory'

The prototype was first registered in February 1949. From this angle the car has a solid, Bentley-type look.

apart from certain engine features which called for improvement.

What Parkes was trying to decide was what sort of performance he wanted from the engine. Within Alvis there were advocates for a hard, fast engine, recalling prewar days, while others pressed for a quieter, more docile power plant, which had smaller valves. The car that Parkes drove most was the second prototype, chassis number 3L2; the engine number is also given as 3L2 rather than a specific series number in the licensing document at Coventry, where it was registered HKV 778.

This prototype was a rather unhappy-looking two-door left-hand-drive estate version of the saloon and had a curious rear section rather like a hearse, which Parkes continued to drive for many years after the Three-litre was in production. It most resembled the Harold Radford Countryman bodies fitted to some Bentley Mark VIs after the war.

Arthur Varney's recollection, which was not shared by Chris Kingham, was that Parkes used to have one of the engines in one of the cars for a couple of weeks and then change it for the other. This happened six or seven times until he took his decision to

The left-hand-drive estate version, much driven by John Parkes. It seems unlikely that the car would have gone into production in this form.

The same car in the service department at Alvis, behind a 12/50 beetleback. The large blind area in the rear quarters is particularly apparent. Note also the ventilator in the roof.

standardize on the 'soft' version. This gave an output of only 86bhp at 3,800rpm, but the aim was to give a good overall power curve – benefiting the lower and middle ranges – rather than a peak performance at high revs.

Varney thought that this basic engine, 'a quiet and docile motor', as he called it, which powered all Alvis production cars from then on, was later spoiled by attempts to extract too much power from it for the Graber versions. Naturally, those who nearly doubled the output of the engine over the next 17 years would disagree.

Apart from tooling costs for the new car, the other major difficulty was the sale price, most particularly the purchase tax element. Between 1945 and 1962 there were no fewer than 10 changes in the tax levels applied to cars. In January 1948, the old licensing tax, which was levied on the notional horsepower of the car based on an abstruse Treasury formula, disappeared to be replaced by a flat £10 Road Fund Licence. However, this deprived the Government of revenue from high-horsepower cars which were naturally the most expensive. As a blunt instrument, the Government doubled the 33.3% purchase tax hitherto applicable to all cars for those costing more than £1,000. This decision had a profound effect on Alvis, which dealt only in the upper price bands and had no range of models like the major manufacturers to help to spread costs.

The distorting effect of this mechanism meant that small manufacturers priced their cars at two pounds under the £1,000 ceiling: the Jaguar 3½-litre, Lea-Francis Fourteen and Alvis TB 14 were all exactly £998; the Armstrong Siddeley Lancaster was a few pounds cheaper. Going over the limit added more than £300 instantly to the cost of the car. While devaluation had helped exports, it also raised the cost of raw materials, so many makers were operating below acceptable profit levels. Although the limit was later raised to £1,250, Parkes was so enraged by this level of tax

The prototype Three-litre chassis, showing clearly the independent front suspension.

Substantial testing of the new six-cylinder engine went on in secret in this Q-car version of the TA 14. The bonnet was lengthened to accommodate the new unit.

that he urged other manufacturers to join Alvis in lobbying the Chancellor of the Exchequer for its removal. He said the tax was a source of 'considerable embarrassment to the present and future plans of many manufacturers'.

It certainly was in the case of Alvis, for Parkes had come to realize that the new Three-litre could only be sold at a level which would attract double tax. There was some talk of cheapening the cost to bring it below the ceiling by reducing the Alvis dealers' margins, but this came to nothing. In addition, Parkes' sums showed that he would have to sell 1,000 cars per year for three years just to amortize the cost of the pressed-steel body. He thought it impractical as production runs of 5,000 or even 10,000 a year might

This first design provided the basis for the engines which were to power Alvis cars for the next 17 years.

be the minimum; on the present factory space and access to capital, this could not be contemplated. The continuing manufacture of cars was, therefore, in his words 'a policy of expediency which would help to absorb overheads'.

By May 1949, the decision was taken to postpone the launch of the new car, on which more than £13,000 had been spent in development costs. The postponement was, in fact, an abandonment of a bold and interesting body design which could have had a dramatic effect on Alvis fortunes. It was also, according to the engine designer Chris Kingham, a 'very, very nice car to drive'. The cancellation was a bitter blow, intensified by the Chancellor's decision a few months later to drop double purchase tax – a decision which would almost have coincided with the launch of the new car.

The prototype 3L1 had engine number 23804 installed before being sold to Central Motors of Sheffield, the reason being that the prototype engines shared the same pistons, crank and con-rods as the production versions, but almost everything else was different, which would have posed a spares problem. The car is believed to have been destroyed in an accident in the Sixties.

John Parkes is thought to have driven the estate version for many years, replacing the prototype engine with a TD 21 unit before the car was scrapped.

Alvis had reached a turning point; though the car division had made a profit – its last ever – in 1948, the company was turning its attention increasingly to aero-engine and other work and away from cars, which had been the main prewar business. Questions were again asked at board level as to whether it was worth continuing, given the latest setback. The decision to continue was taken for two reasons, echoing Parkes' views on expediency: firstly, the car department absorbed some of the overheads from the other contracts, giving the company a competitive edge in negotiating contracts, and secondly, the car business maintained 'prestige and goodwill' for Alvis, particularly in relation to the aviation work. Reasons of history or sentiment played no part in the decision.

However, all was not lost. A first-class 3-litre engine had been developed by Chris Kingham, so had independent front suspension.

A scale version of the Three-litre TA 21, which was to replace the ill-fated pressed-steel project.

Smith-Clarke was very pleased; the top speed and suspension were 'highly satisfactory' and the new package could be put in the new chassis with a body which needed minimal retooling at a cost of only £48,000, to be recovered over a production run of 2,000. Indeed, Smith-Clarke was so pleased with 3L3, which was registered JDU 674, that he subsequently took it into retirement with him.

Again, the question of the body came up; Alvis had decided that they had neither the space nor the staff to build bodies themselves, so back they went to Mulliners. After lengthy haggling, Mulliners were contracted to produce 1,000 saloon bodies at £20 less than the cost of the Fourteen body.

By October 1949 the mock-up was almost ready and by the following summer the first prototype was on the road. The first production Three-litre was panelled in July, though the programme was running two months late due to delays in the delivery of springs.

As the Forties came to an end, there was a fierce debate about the so-called American styling which was creeping into the British motor industry. Perjorative phrases like the 'streamline craze', the 'dollar grin' and the 'mouth-organ look' were hurled around. Parkes, making a virtue out of necessity, said that the Fourteen's replacement – a worthy successor – would be available in mid-1950, and that Alvis had kept keenly in mind the need for 'a traditional English-looking car' rather than one with transatlantic influences. This was rather bold considering that the TB 14 sports was, to put it kindly, a little vulgar for its time, and that the cancelled Three-litre with the pressed-steel body was hardly traditional. However, he had prepared his customers for the fact that the new Alvis saloon would not look radically different from the TA 14 on the stand.

10
SUCCESS
FOR THE SIX

The new Three-litre appeared for the first time at the Geneva show in March 1950. The car had been much discussed as the replacement for the ageing TA 14, and a few months earlier the *London Evening Standard* had incorrectly forecast that it would have a five-speed gearbox and seating for six and would be 'tough and durable for Empire and foreign roads'. Indeed, Geneva had been chosen for the launch in order to give a boost to exports, which was still a major Government priority.

The only picture that had appeared in Britain was a teasing shot of the show car – finished flamboyantly in cream, with tan upholstery and whitewall tyres – disappearing into the back of a railway wagon as it was being loaded for transit to Geneva. In reality it almost disappeared completely, being lost on the European railways for 15 days and nearly missing its debut on the stand. There were even rumours, darkly attributed to foreign competitors, that the car did not exist, but John Parkes drove himself to Geneva in another Three-litre, which suffered water pump and overheating problems – a condition grimly familiar to many Alvis owners.

The Parkes car was used as a demonstrator outside the hall and on a road circuit set aside by the Swiss police. 'We were privileged to handle the car,' said *The Motor* respectfully, 'it is up to the best Alvis traditions in handling qualities: light, high-geared and accurate steering, coupled with a suspension giving a moderately firm ride and first-class roadholding.' The men from *The Motor* forbore to mention at the time that putting the brakes on at speed resulted in a fearful front-end judder as they were charitable enough to believe the problem would go away by the time production versions appeared. Parkes also listened to some criticism of the rear legroom from others, but the new car met with general acclaim – and rightly so. Despite the fact that it was a compromise – a new engine in a basically old body with identical cabin space to the Fourteen – it was a thoroughly civilized carriage and beautifully engineered.

The fairing of the headlights into the front wings and a larger sweep to the rear wings and tail gave it a more modern look than the Fourteen, although it was basically still a prewar design with separate wings, spats covering the rear wheels, removable bonnet sides and a tall radiator topped with a filler cap. Indeed, in side view it bears a startling resemblance to a 1936 prototype design by

The aura of Alvis quality comes through in this factory-posed TA 21 shot, though the impression is slightly spoiled by the ribbed rubber guards on the rear wings. Many were stainless steel.

A poor picture of an important car; JWK 290 was the first works car after the prototypes and had the chassis number 23803. The first production car took the next number.

Walter J Belgrove for a Triumph Dolomite, which was never produced.

Much more attention had been given to making it a car acceptable for export by reducing the amount of wood in the body. The door pillars were cast alloy sections, as was part of the rear wheelarch. This gave a more rigid structure for bad roads and reduced the propensity of the body to warp in hot climates. Mulliners again bought in these sections from outside suppliers. The prewar trademark of the visible spare wheel disappeared and, anticipating modern practice, it was suspended in a tray under the boot floor. Rubber grommets in the front and rear overriders concealed the jacking points, which were direct extensions of the chassis into which fitted a Bevelift jack, which was hard work to operate, despite the handbook illustration of it being achieved effortlessly by an elegant woman.

Although the new car was referred to by Alvis as the Three-litre, it is necessary to distinguish between the various models by using their type designation as the same engine continued through several models until Alvis stopped car production.

The saloon, again built by Mulliners, was the TA 21, the sports roadster was the TB 21 and there was also a drophead coupe by Tickford. All three models were catalogued, very often at the same price, and the practice adopted during the production run of the Fourteen of selling chassis to anyone who would take them to put whatever body they wanted on them, was not repeated, with the notable exception of Hermann Graber.

The saloon had attracted great interest since its launch at Geneva – the other two models had not yet been seen – and by the time of the 1950 Earls Court motor show, when all three were displayed marked 'for export only', there were more than 1,000 orders on the books, though such was the shortage of cars on the home market that people would register their names for a number of models and take the first to arrive. Twenty-nine out of the first 34 delivered had been exported, which not only met export targets, but also exported teething problems a long way from home.

Attention at the show focused mainly on the new 84 x 90mm six-cylinder engine, giving a swept volume of 2,993cc. The engine was almost 'square' in cylinder dimensions, the stroke being not much more than the bore, which made the Fourteen's long-stroke engine look old-fashioned. Although the top speed was quoted as 85mph, the maximum output of 86bhp at 3,800rpm was intended by Chris

The Tickford works at Newport Pagnell, where cars were being prepared for a show. The Alvis in the centre is a hardtop, and according to the man holding the door, Cliff Petts, who worked at Tickford for 50 years, it was the only one the firm ever made.

Kingham to give good torque in the mid-range rather than a high maximum speed, and to provide flexibility in fourth gear. Kingham recalled spending weeks drawing cam profiles and working them out with a slide-rule to give a gentle profile. William Dunn had also given him permission to use cast iron for the crankshaft and camshaft rather than hardened steel, which gave the engine considerable strength. The new car was claimed to be only 50lb heavier than the four-cylinder Fourteen, although it put on more weight as it grew older.

Other notable engine features were a single Solex 30mm dual-downdraught carburettor in the saloon and coupe, feeding polished kidney-shaped combustion chambers. The sparking plugs were angled towards the exhaust valve to give combustion at the hottest point so that pinking could be avoided, which was a particular problem with the Fourteen. The valves themselves were of different sizes, with silicon-chrome steel inlets of 38mm compared with 32mm for the exhausts, providing better breathing, in line with current technology.

The seven-bearing crankshaft ran in thin-wall bearings, driving a duplex roller chain at the rear of the block which turned the high-mounted camshaft. A typically thoughtful touch to enhance smoothness and quiet running was that in addition to the compound valve springs a small spring on each pushrod kept it in constant contact with the rocker, thus transferring mechanical chattering from the overhead valve gear to the bottom of the pushrod, where it was deadened within the block. The substantial cast iron rocker cover also kept noise to a minimum; it is interesting to compare its weight with the flimsy pressings on modern cars.

Though great attention was paid to cooling, with water fed

Another TA 21 hardtop, attributed by some to Tickford, though the shape of the front wings is more expressive of Mulliner of Chiswick.

There must have been a reason for posing this bizarre shot in the Alvis works; it does at least display the Tickford line to good example.

around the cylinder head by an internal copper tube and then directed on to valve seats and plug housings, overheating remained a serious problem for many years until the head was redesigned.

One omission was the lack of an external oil filter. Instead, inside the 12-pint sump floated a wire-mesh intake for the oil pump. The sump itself, an aluminium casting, had to be removed to clean the mesh, which was not particularly fine.

Though many of the external dimensions were similar to those of the Fourteen, the TA 21 was 10in longer and had a wheelbase 3½in larger. The main changes, of course, were beneath, with the new chassis braced by six crossmembers. The largest at the front of the chassis carried the forward engine mountings, the Burman Douglas worm-and-nut steering and the new independent suspension, which had been designed so many years before. Coil springs with dampers and wishbones of unequal length had by now become almost routine on new cars, although subsequently there was a view at Alvis that the designer of the new Three-litre layout had miscalculated the spring rates, for the car tended to be rather soggy at the front despite the rubber-mounted anti-rollbar. Rear suspension was still semi-elliptic with Girling telescopic dampers, although the springs were fitted to the axle asymmetrically, with 22in forward of the axle and 28in behind.

Rod brakes finally disappeared, replaced by Lockheed hydraulic two-leading-shoe type in 11in drums, with a substantial friction area of 189sq in. The handbrake was that deeply unloved feature of the Fifties, the umbrella handle, under the dash, but it did have an 11.5:1 leverage factor as it pulled on a long chassis-pivoted lever which moved the cable to the rear.

The interior had a sense of comfort and refinement, with leather seats, and polished wood on the door cappings and dashboard, which contained a large black speedometer with matching instruments nearby. Sun visors and a sliding roof were standard; the only extras were a radio and, of course, a heater.

The two-seater sports tourer, bodied by AP Panelcraft, was a much better-looking car frontally than its predecessor as it was given the traditional Alvis upright radiator, which blended surprisingly well with its flowing lines. From the radiator back it was very similar to the TB 14, with the wings running through the cutaway doors. Most factory pictures show a fold-flat windscreen, but a fixed, divided screen was standard. Inside, there was a white steering wheel and a dashboard covered in leathercloth, with a large rev-counter driven from the rear of the crankshaft.

There were modifications to give the car a more sporting performance than the saloon and coupe. Although the first car had a single Solex, like the other two models, subsequent cars were fitted with a single horizontal SU 1.75in H6 and a new induction manifold designed to give better gas flow. The cam was slightly altered and the compression ratio was increased from 7:1 in the first models to 7.25:1. There was a higher rear axle ratio and lighter springs at the rear.

Though no contemporary road tests exist, factory data shows that the modified engine had a speed of 20mph per 1,000 revs rather than 18.9, which suggests a top speed of more than 90mph, given that the saloon would hit the mid-80s. Indeed, in 1952 there were hints on the stand at Earls Court from the Alvis salesmen that it would reach the magic 100mph.

The Tickford four-seater coupe, which was on the coachbuilder's stand at Earls Court in 1950 as well as being on Alvis', was the traditionally high-quality, handbuilt carriage with which Tickford had made their reputation. The front of the car back to the scuttle was like the saloon, and it had a three-position hood – closed, coupe-de-ville and open – and a divided bench front seat. Although

Tickford were contracted to build only a drophead, at least one Tickford saloon was built.

The three new models were all catalogued for the motor show at £1,598, which was £300 more than the discontinued Fourteen. Also selling at exactly the same price was the 4-litre Austin A125 Sheerline saloon, and another 'six', the Daimler Consort, cost just a few pounds more. Jaguar were selling their XK 120 and their 3½-litre Mark V at £1,263, but the Bentley Mark VI Standard Steel saloon, which had a resemblance to the Alvis, was more than twice the price at £3,674.

By December 1950, Parkes was able to report at the Alvis annual meeting that orders were flowing in at a high rate, production was increasing steadily and the first deliveries to export distributors were taking place. In fact there were 4,000 orders on the books for the various versions of the Three-litre. What Parkes did not disclose was that the familiar problem of body supplies had returned. Mulliners were failing to deliver the promised 20 bodies per week and those that were arriving were below standard.

By Christmas, Alvis had completed 104 chassis, but there were only 74 saloon bodies to go on them, and Parkes was already agitating for new coachwork to modernize the appearance of the car and reduce the total dependence on Mulliners, whose bodies he was now accepting under protest because there was nowhere else to go if Three-litre saloon production were to continue.

There was also much more profit to be made on the saloon. Given that all three models were listed at the same retail price, Mulliners were charging about £200 a body, AP Metalcraft were providing 100 TB 21 bodies for £342 each and Tickford were charging £350 for a

Stanley Horsfield, the sales manager on the left, with Ron Walton, who wrote the handbook for the Three-litre, outside the factory with a Tickford entrant for the Tulip Rally.

A Tickford with a furled hood at the 1953 Los Angeles show. The poster says that the 'bobby' cannot make an arrest without wearing his striped armband.

run of 300 dropheads. The TB 21 order had been placed to try to open up the United States market, but the Tickford coupe was put into production only because it was realized in June 1950 that Alvis could produce more chassis than Mulliners could body, even if they were delivering to schedule.

The TB 21 project was cut short in the spring of 1951 when purchase tax on cars was doubled to 66.6%. The order for 100 bodies was immediately scaled down to a batch of 30, though few, if any, production versions had been built by this time. In fact, when the car was launched there was not even a proper handbook, only a few typewritten pages to supplement the saloon handbook.

All the models were now catalogued at £1,946 and the TB 21 was £300 more expensive than the Jaguar XK 120, though comparable Healeys, Bristols and Jensens were much dearer. It is a pity that more TB 21s were not built because despite its size, the Alvis was a graceful sports tourer, with effortless cruising power. Production of the other Alvises continued, but in a manner less than smooth. Body problems and difficulties with porous cylinder blocks were experienced, but the order books were full and in June 1951 there were 4,000 of them outstanding. This justified laying down another 1,000 chassis, the target being to make 2,300 in all, of which nearly 2,000 were to be saloons.

Since production began, there had been minor modifications to engine design. The inlet and exhaust manifold gaskets were redesigned after blowing problems and were eventually abandoned altogether for a metal-to-metal fit, which speaks volumes for machining tolerances. Unfortunately, the overheating difficulties were tackled only half-heartedly with water pump improvements and were not addressed properly until a new cylinder head design arrived many years later. Chris Kingham had wanted to replace the head early in the manufacturing cycle, and had designed an overhead-cam version, but the money to put it into production, he remembered ruefully, went instead into a helicopter engine.

At the end of 1951, meanwhile, certain changes were made that led to better engine performance. The Solex carburettor, which was

A sad sight in the service department. The car on the left is probably MWK 180, chassis number 24972. The press, which can be seen over the roof of the middle car, is still in use at Red Triangle.

A factory-posed shot of the TC 21 dash. Note the way the grain is carried across the glovebox lid.

Rear view of the immaculate TB 21, chassis number 25142, which is illustrated in colour on page 11.

prone to dribble fuel when idling, was replaced with twin SU downdraught instruments. The manifolds were redesigned to split the exhausts from cylinders one to three and four to six into separate downpipes and silencers, providing a better path for the gases and reducing exhaust roar. Performance went up to 93bhp at 4,000rpm.

A test by *The Motor* of the saloon in 1952 noted a top speed of 88mph and the ability to reach 75mph in third gear. Speed from 0–50mph was put at 11.2sec and fuel consumption at 19.5mpg. *The Autocar* found it less speedy: 0–50mph in 14.1sec and a long haul to a 0–60mph figure of 19.8sec and a top speed of 86mph. These disparities were probably due to the variable quality of the petrol available at the time, which could cause severe pinking in performance engines.

One unusual TA 21 of the period was car number 24831, supplied without an engine to a Mr Freeman-Sanders of Cornwall. He designed for it his own 2.7-litre six-cylinder diesel engine, which was built by the Camborne engineering firm of Holman. The car, PAF 163, still exists and in 1992 had done only 15,000 miles from new.

Small body changes had been made during the first production run of the TA; early models had horizontal glass ventilating panes at the top of the windows, later the rear window was made larger, and from car number 24653, bumpers of a different section were fitted.

Despite continuing improvements to the car, Parkes had always regarded it as yet another stop-gap model because, although it had many desirable qualities its roots were still firmly in the Thirties. By February 1952 he was reporting to the Alvis directors that urgent modifications were needed, particularly in the width of the bodywork, which had attracted 'widespread criticism'. A prototype of a redesigned body was ordered from Mulliners, with £28,000 put aside for tooling costs. The result of this was probably car number 25330 – which still exists. While retaining the basic TA/TC shape, it has a curved and sloping windscreen, different shaping of the front doors and revised instrumentation. It is believed that this was one of a pair of revised cars, but nothing further seems to have come of the redesign, possibly because another much more important venture, involving Alec Issigonis, was about to begin.

The side profile of the Three-litre was displayed to good effect in this illustration from the company's sales brochure.

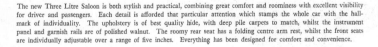
The new Three Litre Saloon is both stylish and practical, combining great comfort and roominess with excellent visibility for driver and passengers. Each detail is afforded that particular attention which stamps the whole car with the hallmark of individuality. The upholstery is of best quality hide, with deep pile carpets to match, whilst the instrument panel and garnish rails are of polished walnut. The roomy rear seat has a folding centre arm rest, whilst the front seats are individually adjustable over a range of five inches. Everything has been designed for comfort and convenience.

11

THE HEALEY HYBRID

The nearest model to a proper Alvis sportscar after the demise of the TB 21 was not an Alvis but a 100mph Healey convertible powered by the Alvis 3-litre engine and gearbox. This hybrid grew from Healey's need to export to the United States and a conversation on board the *Queen Elizabeth* liner between Donald Healey and the president of Nash, who wanted a sporty model in his line-up.

The original model, announced in October 1950, was powered by the American 3.8-litre Nash engine and transmission which came from their Airflyte Ambassador, a bulbous inverted bathtub of a car, which had the distinction of being named in one publication as one of the great cars of the Fifties and in another of being one of the world's worst automobiles. Healey won permission from the Government to import the mechanicals from Kenosha, Wisconsin, on condition that the complete car was exported to the United States for dollars. Although no cars were allowed to be sold on the home market, the model was catalogued and displayed in Britain and it generated a great deal of interest, so much so that Healey decided to produce a version on the same chassis for sale both in Britain and in non-dollar export markets.

In the spring of 1951, Healey asked Alvis for a 3-litre engine for assessment, and in the autumn a very large order arrived at Holyhead Road for 250 3-litre engines and gearboxes to power the chassis being built by Healey at Warwick. There was the prospect of a further outside order, since at the same time Lea-Francis asked for a development engine for a new project; they were quoted £267 each for a batch of 250.

The new G-type Healey had a bodyshell made by Panelcraft of Birmingham, which was trimmed at the Healey works. It appeared for the first time at the London motor show in October 1951, with body revisions to make it more acceptable to a British market – notably a smaller grille than the Nash egg-box and the disappearance of the power bulge on the bonnet, which the Alvis engine did not need.

It was, of course, identical to the TA 21 engine apart from slight modifications to the compression ratio and to cam profiles. With two SU H4 carburettors equipped with pancake filters, power was boosted to 106bhp at 4,200rpm. The external appearance was slightly sportier – the rocker cover had 'Healey' inscribed on the side, and the distributor and plug lead cover, which gave such a

The Alvis-engined Healeys had changes to compression and cam profiles to give better performance than the standard TA 21 engine. This is the chassis number G 505 at a Healey meeting.

smooth appearance to the TA engine, was omitted.

The G-type was considerably faster than the 400lb-heavier standard Alvis saloon. The 0–60mph figure was 13.5sec, according to *The Autocar*, though *The Motor* took only 11.4sec, which they said had been beaten by only three out of 140 cars tested since the war. It was also a true 100mph car, which was still a rarity in those days – although maximum power was being delivered at approximately 86mph road speed, so that at 100mph the engine was beginning to struggle. The great strength of the Alvis engine, as in the TA 21, was in its top gear flexibility because its high torque enabled it to pull smoothly from 10mph in top gear, and then to maintain high average speeds without fuss.

The car itself enjoyed a favourable reception; *The Motor* called it a car of 'quite unusual and exhilarating character' and noted its comfort, three-abreast seating, general standard of furnishings, first-rate roadholding and the sweetness and flexibility of the Alvis engine.

However, sales were far from expectations, and in June 1952 Healey reduced the order from 250 engines to just 21. There was a row between the two car makers about the £3,000 worth of materials which Alvis had bought to fulfil the original order, and eventually a compromise was reached by Healey agreeing to take 41 engines. Yet only some 25 cars were eventually built, with Alvis engine numbers beginning at 25301; it is not known what happened to the other engines. Although the cars are described as Alvis-Healeys, they carried Healey chassis numbers and are therefore not included in Alvis car production totals.

By the end of 1952, dealers were knocking £300 off the list price of £2,490, but this still made it look expensive compared with Alvis' own TB 21 sportster, which had been retailing at £1,945.

For some time Donald Healey had been planning the next generation of cars, which began in 1952 with the 100/4 BN 1, the first of the big Austin-Healeys; Healey did, of course, move eventually to a big 3-litre 'six', but by this time Austin had taken over development and installed their own 3-litre rather than an Alvis engine.

One reason for reducing the original engine order so substantially may well have been reliability problems. Geoffrey Healey remembers 40 years later that there were difficulties with the engine because the Healey sportscar was driven far harder than the Alvis models. He cited piston pickup, poor oil-feed to the valve gear, overheating and cylinder head cracking, which were problems evidenced elsewhere, but perhaps not seen on such a scale.

He did, however, pay tribute to the engine once it had been improved as 'a very fine unit', and Healey continued to enjoy a good relationship with Alvis, taking over some of their toolroom machines to make spare parts at Warwick for older Alvis models, thus freeing factory space at Coventry for the current cars.

More than half of the 25 Alvis-Healeys still survive; the Nash version was more successful as over 500 were built, with the last of the run being bodied by Pinin Farina. The Anglo-US sportscar collaboration continued with the Bertone-bodied Arnolt-Bristol and later the AC Cobra, but Alvis' involvement was limited to the export of the home-grown TB 21 and, later, the Graber models.

12

ISSIGONIS AND THE V8

Alec Issigonis had made his name at the Nuffield Organisation with his Morris Minor, although in 1952 the eventual success that this car would achieve was little appreciated. However, Nuffield's merger that year with Austin drove him away from Morris when it became clear that the Austin staff at Longbridge would have the upper hand in future engineering design rather than their opposite numbers at Nuffield's Cowley headquarters.

Donald Healey had told him that Alvis were on the point of designing a new car, and so, on June 5, 1952, after an interview with Parkes, Alec Arnold Issigonis signed a five-year contract with Alvis as engineer/designer at a salary of £2,500 a year. The lengthy document assigned all rights in his inventions on behalf of the company to Alvis and swore him to secrecy about the new project, initially codenamed TA 175/350. Rowland Simmons, who worked in the service department at the time, recalled that the project aroused great curiosity in the works. There was much tip-toeing to the back of the test-house to catch a glimpse of the car through the window.

Issigonis began work, with the grand title of Engineer-in-Charge of Passenger Car Design, in a room which contained just two drawingboards and two ashtrays and was situated next door to the design department at Holyhead Road. At the other board sat the engine designer Chris Kingham, and they were shortly to be joined by a small group which included Harry Barber and John Sheppard. They moved soon afterwards to the basement where they became known as 'the cell' because of their location and isolation from the rest of the company.

Issigonis' brief was to look into the future for Alvis and to design a new car with a new engine. The codename stood for the 1,750cc and 3,500cc V8 size of the engines. They were to power a sporting family car which was to bear the Issigonis trademark of being compact, wide and light – weighing 25cwt (2,800lb). It was to be just over 13ft long, but a full five-seater. The initial plan was for 5,000 cars to be built per year for five years, but Colonel Chaytor, one of the more bullish directors, wanted a production rate of 10,000 per year, which was a huge volume by Alvis standards, especially as their existing annual capacity was only 2,000 cars.

Arthur Varney, although by then working on the aero-engine side, was asked by Parkes to keep a daily eye on Issigonis so as to help him to get to know the factory and make him feel at home. Many years later he recalls: 'I can remember Issigonis saying that his ideal of a small car was one which was a box with a wheel on each corner. I told him of a 1,000cc car we had designed which had front-wheel drive, had the engine across the chassis and the gearbox behind it.

'This intrigued Issigonis enormously; he asked if he could see the drawings, but I had to tell him that they had all been destroyed in the Blitz. I often wonder how much that conversation contributed towards the Mini concept.'

It would be a pleasing thought that a prewar Alvis prototype had inspired the Mini, but according to Gerald Palmer, designer of the Jowett Javelin and the Riley Pathfinder, who worked with Issigonis at Morris, Issigonis had already been working on the idea before he joined Alvis. Palmer finished off a transverse-engine Minor with front-wheel drive which Issigonis had been experimenting upon before he left.

Issigonis' method of operation was to make sketches, which he then worked upon continuously with the draughtsmen, doing overlays so as to achieve the design which pleased him. It was from these that the production drawings were made.

Although a 1,750cc engine was part of the Alvis brief, it was probably not drawn and certainly was never made; it would perhaps have comprised one bank of the V8, which itself was constructed only in experimental form, with all the castings and machining done in-house at Alvis. It was an all-aluminium design with the two four-cylinder banks set at 90deg, each with a single overhead camshaft driven by shaft and bevel gears. Apart from the valvegear, it must have borne more than a passing resemblance to the Buick 3.5-litre V8 engine which much later was used to such good effect by Rover.

There were two unusual developments in the project, which by this time was known only as the TA 350. The first was a two-speed gearbox mounted on the rear axle, linked to an electrically-operated Laycock overdrive under the front seats, giving four speeds in all. The gear-lever was on the right-hand side of the front bench seat and the clutch was a Smiths Selectdrive unit. Although the differential was a standard Salisbury unit it was fitted into a special casing which also contained an Alvis-made two-speed gearbox. As the engine had considerable torque, the low gearbox ratio would be suitable for town use and the high ratio for sustained speeds, with the overdrive adding flexibility.

The second, and most significant innovation was the independent suspension designed by Alex Moulton. Working with Jack Daniels, Issigonis' assistant in Morris days, he had originally used rubber in torsion, which he called Flexitor, with great success in one of the Morris Minor prototypes. The concept had impressed Issigonis, who was himself an expert in suspension design, although it was too late in the design cycle to incorporate it into the Minor. Issigonis and Moulton became not only colleagues, but friends, and Moulton, whose family firm manufactured rubber components, sold him the idea of using rubber-cone suspension named Diabolo, so-called because back-to-back the rubber cones looked like the ancient two-headed diabolo top which was spun on string suspended between two sticks.

However, new interconnected forms of suspension were being mooted by Citroen and Packard, and after much joint work between Moulton and Issigonis, the rubber cones were filled with water and linked by hoses front-to-rear. This had the effect of averaging out bumps by displacing the fluid from one set of rubber cones to another. This was the first use ever made of a system which developed into the Hydrolastic suspension used by BMC, firstly in

The contract signed by Alec Issigonis in June 1952, when he was taken on to design a new generation of cars for Alvis. An addendum signed on November 30, 1955, after the cancellation of the project, released him from its provisions other than to keep Alvis' secrets and to hand over any inventions.

This Agreement

made the fifth day of June One thousand nine hundred and fiftytwo BETWEEN ALVIS LIMITED whose registered office is at Holyhead Road Coventry in the County of Warwick (hereinafter called "the Company") of the one part and ALEC ARNOLD ISSIGONIS of Flat No.6 Linkside Avenue Oxford in the County of Oxford (hereinafter called "Mr. Issigonis") of the other part

WHEREBY IT IS HEREBY AGREED as follows:

1.   The Company shall employ Mr. Issigonis and Mr. Issigonis shall serve the Company (subject as hereinafter provided) as an Engineer/Designer for the term of FIVE YEARS from the first day of May One thousand nine hundred and fiftytwo and thereafter unless and until determined by either party giving to the other not less than three calendar months' notice in writing expiring at any time.

2.   Mr. Issigonis shall devote his whole time and attention to his duties hereunder and shall well faithfully and diligently serve the Company and use his utmost endeavours to promote the interests thereof and shall not without the consent of the Board during the term of his employment hereunder be engaged concerned or interested directly or indirectly in any other trade business or employment.   Provided always that nothing in this clause shall prohibit Mr. Issigonis from holding shares debentures or other securities of any other Company by way of bona fide investment only.

3.   Mr. Issigonis shall carry out such duties in relation to engineering and design work as shall be assigned to him by the Board or the Managing Director and shall in the discharge of such duties observe and perform all lawful orders and directions from time to time made or given to him by the Board or the Managing Director.

4.   Mr. Issigonis shall receive by way of remuneration for his services a fixed salary at the rate of two thousand five hundred pounds per annum during the first three years of this Agreement and at the rate of three thousand pounds per annum thereafter and which shall be payable by equal monthly instalments in arrear on the last day of each calendar month.

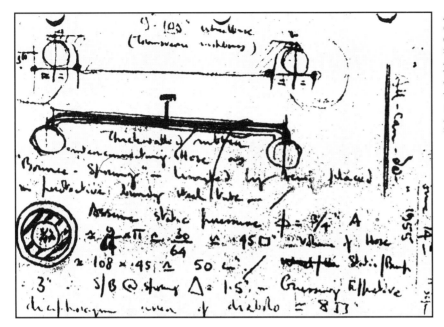

Alex Moulton's original drawings for the fluid-connected suspension system in the Issigonis Alvis, showing the rubber tubing linking the two wheels and a section through the hose. The principle pioneered at Alvis has gone on to suspend millions of cars.

the 1100 cars in 1962 and latterly, in Hydragas form, in the Allegro and Rover Metro.

Thirty years after his pioneering design for the TA 350, Moulton estimated that his rubber cones had suspended 6 million cars. He described his first Alvis test drive as an 'absolute revelation'; the fluid interconnection system gave the car slow-acting suspension, or what he called 'a big-car ride'. A similar long-wheelbase car, like the Lancia Aprilia, with conventional suspension, gave a quick, jerky ride. Rowland Simmons, who then worked in the service department, drove the car several times and was full of praise: 'It went around corners as if it were on rails.'

The least remarkable feature of the car was the body. Only drawings now seem to exist, but those who saw it remember it being dumpy. Gerald Palmer remarked that the car looked very pedestrian in design. Issigonis himself likened it to a Lancia Aurelia, although he admitted that since Alvis could not afford a stylist like Farina, the design was done by themselves. Despite its looks, it was a compact car, which was very spacious inside, with hardly any intrusion from the propeller-shaft tunnel. The radiator grille – originally a wide bar across the width of the car, but later redesigned after protests from the sales department – lifted up with the bonnet, like the Wolseley Hornet would in the Sixties, and the rear wings were bolted on. Moulton called it a very simple, basic car, contesting a view in some circles that it looked like an inflated Morris Oxford. He remembered that its long wheelbase and wide track drew most of the attention. Yet he said it looked completely unstyled, like an engineering drawing.

Issigonis reckoned that with 130bhp in the final version, and a very favourable power-to-weight ratio, two speeds with overdrive were sufficient. It was certainly fast, and according to John Parkes, although not highly tuned, had lapped at 105mph on the test track at the Motor Industry Research Association establishment near

Nuneaton 'without being pressed'. During the day it was locked out of sight in a shed there; after dark it was the practice for the small team, including the draughtsmen, to drive on the track night after night, sometimes clocking up, as Mike Parkes did, 1,000 miles in 10 hours, even though his father, John Parkes, had forbidden him to have anything to do with the project.

The original engine design was soon altered. The first V8 had a barrel crankcase like the Miller racing engines, but Issigonis, who had insisted on it, later called this a 'ghastly mistake' because it could not be kept quiet. There were problems of differential expansion in the crankcase and the crank rattled in its bearings. Horizontal bolts were put through the crankcase to eliminate play, but Chris Kingham called the unit an unstable disaster; he redrew the design with the help of the Alvis foundry manager to make it more conventional, recalling that the foundry made an excellent job of working with him on the aluminium castings.

The other major change was in the cylinder heads. Bill Cassels, who worked on the project with Issigonis, remembered that the camshafts were originally in tunnels. The shafts were slid inside before the heads were bolted down, and once this was done there was no means of adjusting the tappets. Issigonis apparently believed that it would not need to be done, but after a few hours' running the engine sounded like 'a bag of nails' according to Cassels, and the heads were redesigned to give access to the inverted bucket tappets. There had also been two intake manifolds; the first was called 'the octopus' because of the maze of pipes leading into the engine from the single SU carburettor. Despite the difficulty of feeding eight cylinders, the set-up gave nearly 100bhp. However, Issigonis wanted more, and two SUs and a different manifold were fitted, giving more than 125bhp. By November 1953, the engine had completed 300 hours of testing.

Two years after beginning the project, Issigonis reported to the board that there were still minor mechanical problems, but the only serious defect was the directional stability of the car. However, by the end of 1954 there had been an extensive redesign of not only the engine, but also the transmission because of propeller-shaft balance problems; the final car had a split shaft with a centre bearing. The suspension had also been modified from the original dry-cone system through a system of balloons under fluid pressure to the final fluid interconnection. The final prototype for demonstration was expected by the spring of 1955.

The Issigonis Alvis, which presumably had run on trade plates during testing, was registered PVC 835 in Coventry on February 12, 1955. The registration document was discovered by the indefatigable registrar of the Alvis Owner Club, Dave Culshaw, who trawled through 30,000 Coventry index cards to find the entry which specifies a saloon body, maroon in colour, with a chassis/engine number of TA 501. A certain amount of road-testing was done in great secrecy. Moulton recalled being summoned on occasion to 'Point X', somewhere outside Cirencester, where the testing began.

To fool the opposition, the car had a cardboard octagon taped over on the nose, to that the inquisitive might think it was an MG prototype. However, if they had looked inside they would have seen the Alvis logo on the speedometer.

Had the car gone into production, most of the components would have been bought-in and Alvis might not even have made the engine as specifications were sent to the lorry builders Maudslay for assessment. At this time Alvis were doing a lot of sub-contract work for Rolls-Royce, so it might have made sense to use the company's first-class production facilities for this lucrative work and have the engine made elsewhere. There was even discussion about building a new 75,000sq ft factory, possibly outside Coventry, where labour would be cheaper.

At the project's outset the decision had been taken to make the body from steel pressings rather than have it coachbuilt, and accordingly the Pressed Steel Company were to begin tool design in August 1954 to fulfil the Alvis plan of exhibiting the new car at the 1956 London motor show. From then on, there was to be a production run of 2,000 cars per year for three years, which was much scaled down from the original bold plans. The intention was to sell the car at the same £1,250 price as the Three-litre (purchase tax having come down again), but to make more money from it because the Pressed Steel body would be cheaper than the Mulliner saloon; it would cost £118 in white, untrimmed, and £225 as a finished, painted body.

However, the Alvis board were still not convinced that 2,000 cars per year could be sold and so delayed the initial tooling order that Pressed Steel moved the date for the start of work to the end of 1955, which meant that the new car would not appear before the beginning of 1958.

John Parkes suggested that Pressed Steel should proceed anyway, without a definite commitment, but they were not prepared to do this. Parkes had had the prototype tested by outsiders, who spoke highly of its performance and design, but his own view was that the car was not sufficiently advanced to commit Alvis to volume production.

There was also a major financial problem looming: Alvis' bankers had refused to lend any money to launch the new car and only £300,000 could be raised from the company's own resources. It was originally estimated that to produce 2,500 cars per year selling at £950 plus tax would require capital of £1 million, though doubling the cost of the car and reducing the volume to 500 per year would just about cover costs.

The final blow came in June 1955. Pressed Steel, who had originally estimated body tooling costs at between £350,000 and £375,000, announced that due to increased charges for labour and materials, tooling would now cost £620,000. In addition, the bodies would cost £233 each and they would not consider production of fewer than 100 per week, which was far in excess of what Alvis believed could be sold. The works director's revised costings estimated that the capital expenditure required for producing 5,000 cars per year would be £2.5 million, or £1 million to produce 2,000 per year.

A last-ditch attempt was made to find a smaller supplier. Singer said they could make 40 bodies per week with an investment of £300,000 for tooling, but they were unable to give a price for individual bodies other than pointing out that their own SM 1500 body cost them £365. The Issigonis team looked at other alternatives to pressed steel, including the use of plywood to form a body – a technique used in the Mosquito aircraft and later in the Marcos car.

However, it was all over; the money could not be found and 'after prolonged discussion and with great reluctance', Alvis abandoned the Issigonis car in June 1955, though there was no public announcement. Four months later *The Birmingham Post* was still reporting that the car would be delayed for the time being. On the eve of the Paris motor show it said that there was regret that the eagerly-awaited car would not appear.

The team were were bitterly disappointed; Chris Kingham said they felt they had an exciting and attractive package, with a very rugged engine. Moulton was released from his contract to give exclusivity on his suspension designs to Alvis, and on November 17, 1955, Issigonis was given a month's notice; the next day he met Leonard Lord of BMC, who offered him a job at Longbridge, a decision he agonized over for some time before accepting.

He took some of his work with him when he left. His first project at BMC was the XC9001, a medium-sized car which was to use an aluminium 1.5-litre overhead-cam engine – one bank of the Alvis V8. Yet this, too, was fated; the Suez crisis brought it to an end and Lord insisted on a small car in its place, which became the Mini. The only remnant of the TA 350 which survived and was incorporated was Moulton's original rubber-cone suspension.

Alex Moulton, outside his workshops in Bradford-upon-Avon, showing a sectioned version of the original Alvis suspension unit, which displays clearly the rubber sphere in which the fluid was contained.

BMC said they were prepared to buy the prototype TA 350, but Parkes refused to sell it since what BMC were prepared to offer bore no relation to the £76,186 cost of the project – more than three quarters of a million pounds at Nineties prices. Therefore the car, or cars, were put into storage at Broad Lane.

There may well have been more than one version other than PVC 835. The registration documents for the numbers either side are missing, and Arthur Varney remembered there being three 'very clean, very well-polished and nicely upholstered' cars, though Chris Kingham and others thought that there was only one runner. Kingham remembered the runner being pushed into a room with no windows, where the suspension systems were removed and taken to BMC, and the body supported on trestles. The body fixtures were piled on the roof, which eventually collapsed.

According to Rowland Simmons, the car stood there for a long time until a reorganization, when the shop was being cleared out and the space was needed. The works director, Mr Nixon, told a maintenance engineer to get rid of the car. On a Saturday morning it was taken to a piece of wasteland where it was then cut up with a torch.

While he may well have been disappointed at the time by the collapse of the Alvis project, Issigonis seems to have had second thoughts. He told *The Motor* many years later: 'I'm glad it didn't happen; I was never happy with that car, you know.'

Mike Parkes put one of the two engines in a plywood special, though it was never completed, and the other went, for a time at least, to Aston Martin for assessment.

One intriguing sidelight on the affair is the interest shown in the TA 350 by David Brown, who owned both Aston Martin and Lagonda, which he had bought in 1947 to get hold of Bentley's remarkably potent twin-overhead-camshaft 2.6-litre engine, which had been designed in 1943 by Willie Watson.

Brown had known Issigonis for a number of years and was impressed with what he had heard about Alvis' secret car and particularly its high-performance engine.

The Issigonis Alvis as it might have been. No photographs are known to exist, but Brian Hatton's fine reconstruction based on line drawings and other information reveals the body profile and the design's typically Issigonis long wheelbase. Picture courtesy of *Classic and Sportscar.*

In February 1954, he and a director of Alvis met at a London club to discuss co-operation in manufacturing and marketing between Alvis and Aston Martin-Lagonda, a subject which had been touched on tentatively in the past and was now of more interest to Brown as he had acquired a 10% stake in Alvis. The Alvis man reported back that Brown had said he would very much like to market the sportscar side of their new job, but that if he had a stake in the business, he preferred to control the policy. He went on to suggest a merger, or a takeover of Alvis, which alarmed the Alvis man, who pointed out that the company preferred to remain independent, that no positive plans had been made for the TA 350 and that Brown might be mistaken if he thought Alvis were going ahead with it.

Brown later invited Parkes to stay at his country house in Yorkshire and took him on a tour of his gearbox and tractor works in Huddersfield, for he was interested not only in the TA 350, but in integrating the engineering side of the two firms. It was Sir David Brown's recollection nearly half a century later that Parkes himself would have welcomed a merger, but the Alvis board could not be persuaded, and eventually Parkes relayed the message that Alvis wanted to remain independent and that the intervention of outside interests might be an embarrassment. Brown's reply was to offer to sell his Alvis holdings, but he also declared that he was ready to take over development of the Issigonis car; failing that, the two companies might consider co-operating on tooling and body supplies. Nothing further came of the approach and Brown did eventually sell the Alvis shares – at a profit, he remembered, as they had risen in value because of takeover talk.

It is interesting to speculate on Brown's interest in the Alvis V8. At that time his stylish Lagonda coupe was powered by a 3-litre 'six', which was also offered in the DB2/4 with the added option of Bentley's 2.6-litre engine.

At a remove of years, Sir David was certain that had he bought the TA 350 engine one of the other two would have had to go, but was not sure which one because comparable calculations on power/weight ratios had not been done. Possibly his plan would have been for the V8 to power a new generation of Astons.

However, the Aston works at Feltham, in Middlesex, were unimpressed with the Issigonis engine given to them for assessment. The V8 had been taken there in great secrecy, having been transported by lorry in the middle of the night and then run on the test-bed.

Harold Beach, Aston's engine designer and later technical director, thought it poor: 'It had a dreadful crankshaft like a piece of bent wire. We had no use for it and sent it back to Alvis.' What happened to it then remains a mystery, though it seems likely that it was destroyed.

There was to be a further twist. In January 1955, David Brown took over Tickford as he needed a bodybuilder for his Astons. Alvis were told that the Newport Pagnell coachbuilders would make no more drophead coupes on the Three-litre chassis other than those already ordered; there had originally been 400 orders and the last models were nearing completion. The reason given for the decision was 'other commitments'.

However, Tickford workers were taken aback, as Cliff Petts, who was there at the time, remembered: 'We liked working on the Alvis and couldn't understand why the work stopped as we were left with not a lot to do.'

It was not to be the end of discussions between Alvis and the David Brown Corporation, however, as these resumed some years later with a similar suggestion.

13

THE GREY LADY – TC 21/100

While development of the Issigonis car continued, sales of the Three-litre were falling. Orders were down partly because the model was beginning to look so dated and partly because of uncertainty over purchase tax changes, and by the end of 1952, cars were being sent to dealers in the United Kingdom on a sale-or-return basis. To enable production to continue, more cars were sent to the United States, 80 going in a year to New York and Los Angeles. After a while the Alvis dealer in Los Angeles, Cavalier Motors, wrote complaining of 'an excessive stock of cars' which they could not sell, and asked if they could return seven Tickford coupes and a saloon. The sales director, Stanley Horsfield, was sent to the West Coast to explain that Alvis did not want them back, and managed to persuade the New York distributor, Fergus Motors, to take six of them. One of the traditional Alvis markets, Australia, was still closed to imports, and it was estimated that despite the sales department's efforts only 10% of Three-litre production was going overseas by 1952.

However, the longer-term record was more creditable. Of the total production of the TA series of some 1,300 cars, nine chassis, 184 saloons and 112 dropheads went abroad. The balance of the cars which remained in Britain was 819 saloons and 190 dropheads.

Although the Alvis was always regarded as a sporting car, there was only a limited amount of factory participation in rally events. A TA 21, MLY 913, took part in the Tulip Rally in 1952, but was not in the class results. The following year, three ladies – Nancy Mitchell, Dorothy Stanley-Turner and Rosemary Fotheringham-Parker – set off from Glasgow on the Monte Carlo Rally in LWK 226, but they failed to finish.

However, in 1955 there was success for Ronnie Adams from Northern Ireland and Denis Wilkins, who took part in the RAC Rally. Their TC 21, OWK 605, came fourth in the general classification, first in the class over 2,000cc and was fastest in class in the tests on the Goodwood and Oulton Park circuits and on the Prescott hillclimb. The same car, equipped with a third windscreen wiper among other refinements, was used by *The Autocar* to cover the Monte earlier in the year and they reported themselves to be very impressed with it.

In early 1953 the TA was given a slight facelift to modernize its appearance. It had already been renamed the TC 21, in which form

Opposite page, one of two Grey Lady drophead coupes by Tickford, both supplied by the London Alvis distributor, Brooklands. The other car is pictured in colour on page 13.

There's an air of quality about the polished walnut dashboard with its neat arrangement of driving controls and instrument dials—the ideal background for the sleekly modern steering wheel and column.

In the extra-spacious boot, with the tools handily carried along the right side, there's room enough for a whole load of luggage, and tucked away beneath the luggage boot is the spare wheel tray which can be simply let down without disturbing a single suitcase.

TC 21/100

SALOON

PRICE

TC 21/100 Saloon .. £1,285
plus £536 10s. 10d. purchase tax

it had a different fuel tank from the TA and an improved exhaust system, and at a slightly earlier stage twin SU carburettors had been introduced.

Then, in the spring of 1953, around about car number 25380, it gained a more pleasing appearance from the side. The rather old-fashioned heavy door frames were replaced by concealed-hinge doors hung on a narrower central pillar, and the window frames themselves were made thinner and were plated rather than painted. Quarter-lights were fitted in the rear windows as well as those at the front. There were also a handful of Graber specials and a few Tickford dropheads on the same chassis.

Despite the changes to the saloon, the need for a new model was still urgent, yet the Issigonis car could not appear at Earls Court before 1955 at the earliest. Stanley Horsfield believed that loyal Alvis customers would still buy the diminishing production of the TC 21 in the meantime, but his real concern was that with fewer sales the Alvis dealer network would fall totally into the hands of the Bix Six manufacturers, so that when the new car came along there would be no-one to sell it.

The problem of improving the Three-litre sales was solved by emphasizing performance and giving it a slightly sportier look, for

This is how the company promoted the Grey Lady saloon in the car's sales brochure.

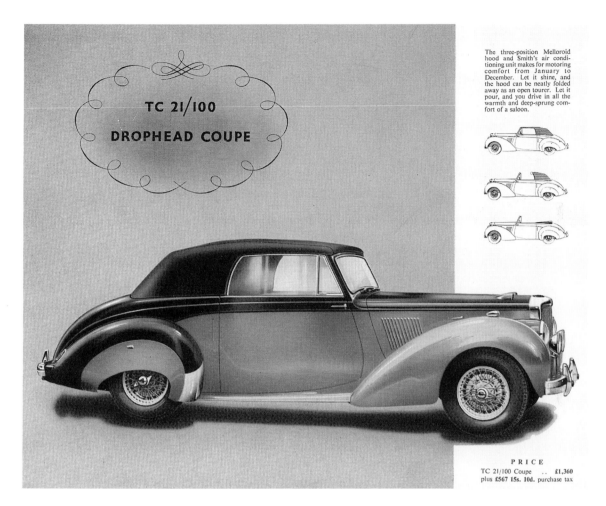

TC 21/100

DROPHEAD COUPE

The three-position Melloroid hood and Smith's air conditioning unit makes for motoring comfort from January to December. Let it shine, and the hood can be neatly folded away as an open tourer. Let it pour, and you drive in all the warmth and deep-sprung comfort of a saloon.

PRICE
TC 21/100 Coupe .. £1,360
plus £567 15s. 10d. purchase tax

An illustration of the drophead coupe version of the Grey Lady taken from the same brochure.

which Horsfield claimed the credit. Thus the famous Grey Lady was born, shown for the first time at the Earls Court motor show in 1953 on both the Alvis and the Mulliners stands. The former exhibit was one of the few cars to be named after its colour, being grey in paintwork and trim, although the car on the Mulliners stand was finished in blue and black.

The official designation was TC 21/100, the latter figure being a heavy reference to the bhp and to the top speed which the Three-litre could now achieve. Indeed, in *The Motor* price list, which put it at £1,821 − £50 more than the standard TC saloon − it was described as 'TC 21/100 (100mph) saloon'.

In the Fifties, there was still a magic about 'the ton', which could be reached on mean maximum speed by only a very few cars. Only five out of the 33 cars tested by *The Autocar* in 1953 achieved this, these being the Frazer-Nash Targa Florio, the Aston-Martin DB2/4, the Austin-Healey 100, the Bentley Continental and the TC 21/100. The Grey Lady, though sounding staid, was in very fast company.

There was a feeling that the car really needed a new cylinder head, and some small modifications had been made, but the improvements in performance were achieved by fairly simple methods, most of which had already appeared on the standard

TC 21. The engine, with an 8:1 compression ratio, now delivered a robust 100bhp at 4,000rpm compared with 86bhp at 3,800rpm in the original TA 21. The rear axle ratio was 3.77:1 compared with 4.09.

Externally, the main differences in some, but not all, of the cars were the Dunlop centre-lock wire wheels and two bonnet-scoop air intakes which not only helped the breathing of the twin SUs, but also ducted in cooling air to reduce underbonnet temperatures. Bonnet sides were louvred to assist the process. A heater came as standard, as did Lucas Flarepath long-range fog and driving lamps and Trico windscreen washers. A motif inscribed with either 'TC 21/100' or 'Grey Lady' was available for the bonnet sides.

Horsfield achieved something of a marketing coup with the Grey Lady, for the bonnet scoops and wire wheels were no more than a contemporary version of 'go-faster' stripes. The 'new' car was basically the same mechanically as the standard TC 21, of which nearly 200 had been built before the Grey Lady was launched.

The Three-litre brochure initially described the saloon as being available with either the 7:1 or 8:1 compression ratio engine, presumably while stocks of the TA unit were being used up, and here confusion arises. The 8:1 ratio was standard in the TC 21/100, but many other TC 21s were later retrofitted with the 8:1 unit. The brochure boasted that 'speeds in excess of 90mph are easily obtainable without any sacrifice of the exceptional flexibililty and virile powers of acceleration which have always characterized this classic among British cars'. It does seem that the only substantial

A striking picture taken at the factory of a TC 21/100. The bonnet motif says 'Grey Lady', though the 'TC 21/100' motif was also available. The van just visible in the background is sign-written 'Alvis Ltd Coventry'.

Though Alvis did not seek competition success with any enthusiasm, this TC 21, driven by Ronnie Adams and Denis Wilkins, was fourth overall in the 1955 RAC Rally and was best in class at Goodwood and Oulton Park. The car had been used by *The Autocar* earlier in the year to cover the Monte Carlo Rally; the third windscreen wiper was installed at that time.

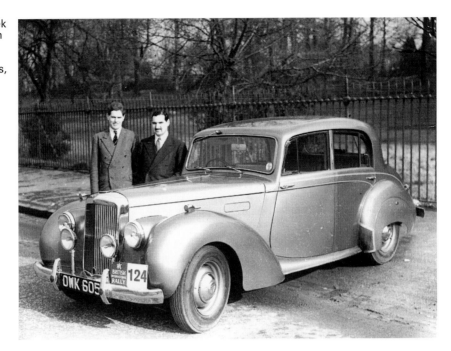

mechanical difference was the fitting of the 3.77:1 rear axle to the TC 21/100 from car 25421, rather than the 4.09:1 which was in the standard car as late as 25380.

Horsfield's strategy worked, for the Earls Court launch drew considerable attention to the car, which received a warm reception. Contemporary road tests spoke of the traditional Alvis values of build quality and comfort. Harold Hastings, whose *The Motor* also described it as a sportscar 'that enjoys being hurried', recalled years later the relief at Alvis when the magazine's road test showed that it had passed the 100mph barrier, even if it was only by one-tenth of a second!

John Bolster in *Autosport* complained about the dip switch and the lack of a rev-counter, although he praised the car as one which wanted to go fast – 0–60mph in 14.6sec – and as extremely pleasant to drive, while remaining thoroughly practical.

Alvis publicity material later drew attention to the fact that the car could pull from 10mph to 100mph in top gear: 'Everybody – Press, agents and customers alike – are intrigued with the docile performance on top gear, even down to a mere crawl.'

There were now three models: the Grey Lady saloon at £1,821, the standard saloon, which looked exactly like the Grey Lady except for its wire wheels and bonnet modifications, and retailed at £1,771, and the Tickford drophead, which was the most expensive model at £1,848.

Production of the TC 21 stopped after some 280 chassis had been built and the TC 21/100 probably started at around chassis number 25421, running through to 25908, with occasional standard TC 21s in between. There were problems with erratic deliveries of saloon bodies from Mulliners. At one stage the London distributor, W F Bates, who ran Brooklands of Bond Street, became so frustrated that he asked for 50 to 100 chassis so that he could arrange for other coachwork to be built on them. His request was rejected because the materials would have cost Alvis £18,000.

At the 1954 Earls Court show, Horsfield, ever the optimist, reported marked interest in the Grey Lady and very few service complaints from owners. However, because of the paucity of supplies of the Grey Lady, there were fears that some Alvis distributors would not renew their contracts.

Then came the latest in a series of literal body blows which Alvis was to suffer during the postwar period. With the spread of unitary construction in the motor industry, bodybuilding firms were being taken over by the giants, and in October 1954, Standard-Triumph at Canley entered an agreement with Mulliners for sole production of bodies. Mulliners had already been producing batch bodies for Standard for some years, and in 1958 were absorbed into the empire.

The 1954 agreement meant that there would be no more saloon bodies for Alvis. The last body was Mulliners number 3599, and worse was to follow in 1955 when Tickford was taken over by Aston Martin. At the time of the Mulliners deal, hopes were still high of the Issigonis V8, but when they were dashed the car business of Alvis looked as if it were facing extinction.

When production of the TC series came to an end in 1955, 725 chassis, more than 400 Grey Ladies, 101 Tickford convertibles and 26 Grabers had been built; the rest were Mulliners saloons. The car division was losing considerable amounts of money. The finance director told the board that the losses could be justified only to preserve goodwill and trade relations until the Issigonis car arrived, though Alvis as a whole was profitable due to the aero-engine and other businesses.

Three-litre production was detailed in the Alvis papers in just over four years as: 2,088 chassis, of which 1,600 including pre-production bodies were used for saloons, 400 including 100 built on the TC21/100 chassis were used for the coupe and 30 were used on the sports version, making a total of 2,030.

Alvis car numbering is not an exact science, since there was a considerable overlap and variation in apportioning chassis numbers. However, the total above is as close as can reasonably be attained. The other chassis numbers were accounted for by various uses, notably those being bodied by Hermann Graber in Switzerland, and allocated to Alvis engines on Healey chassis.

The Grey Lady appeared for the last time at Earls Court in 1955, priced at £1,821. The sensation of the show was the new Jaguar 2.4 selling at £1,269, but on the Alvis stand was a car which was to assure the company's future as a car maker for the next decade and more.

14

THE GRABER CONNECTION

The Swiss coachbuilding industry was small and devoted to those customers who could afford specialist and often beautiful bodywork on conventional chassis, which did not mirror some of the excesses of the French carrosserie like Figoni et Falaschi. Having no indigenous car industry, the Swiss builders worked on chassis from all over the world for their wealthy clients.

Their doyen was undoubtedly Hermann Graber of Witrach, in Berne. Over a period of 45 years he built bodies on chassis as varied as those of Duesenberg and Bugatti, and all were executed with a considerable sense of line and style, eschewing the over-use of chrome and taking great care over the furnishings and fittings of his cars.

His connection with Alvis began after the war when he imported the Fourteen chassis on which he built three Tropic coupes. When the TA 21 was announced, he took some of the first production chassis and displayed a drophead at the Geneva show in 1951 and 1952. The following year he showed a closed coupe, which in 1992 was in the possession of the noted Alvis aficionado Nick Simpson, who rescued it from dilapidation in Switzerland. These models had a grace and purity of line which made the TA/TC series look very staid, and they attracted much attention. Graber ordered 30 chassis a year for the next two years in order to meet the demand.

The first suggestion that Graber might do more than build one-off bodies on Alvis chassis was made by the redoubtable London distributor W F Bates, of Brooklands, who was perpetually pushing Alvis for more cars. He proposed to sales manager Stanley Horsfield that Graber-bodied cars would be a useful addition to the Alvis range at home and abroad. The proposal reached the Alvis board in April 1954, but it was rejected as impracticable because it was thought that there would not be a worthwhile market for a car at the price. At the time the decision probably seemed sensible as the Issigonis car was still being developed and the Mulliners body supplies were not threatened.

However, in the following year, when it looked as if car production might have to be halted for good because of the loss of body facilties at both Mulliners and Tickford, new thinking took place. There were plans to display a Swiss-built Graber coupe on the Alvis stand at both the London and Paris motor shows in the autumn of 1955. Two right-hand-drive TC 21/100 cars with Graber

ALVIS 3 litres Cabriolet 4-5 places carrossé par GRABER

possède le même châssis éprouvé et le même moteur que le coupé. Sa spacieuse carrosserie offre place à 4 ou 5 personnes; ses larges portières assurent un accès aisé, même aux sièges du fond. L'aménagement intérieur, aussi raffiné que celui du coupé, est confectionné exclusivement à l'aide de cuir de première qualité. L'encadrement mince du pare-brise et les étroits piliers procurent des conditions de visibilité parfaites. La capote, dont la face intérieure est doublée avec soin, fonctionne de manière semi-automatique et n'exige aucun effort, grâce à son équilibrage à ressorts; ouverte, elle se dissimule entièrement dans la carrosserie. Splendide voiture de tourisme et de sport quand elle est découverte, elle est aussi confortable et douillette qu'une limousine une fois fermée.

ALVIS 3 litres en Cabriolet 2-3 places Sport spécial

Cette voiture sportive carrossée par GRABER possède le même moteur et le même châssis. Elle répond aux exigences de l'automobiliste qui désire une voiture de sport sans renoncer au confort et comprend deux larges places à l'avant, puis deux places de secours utilisables pour le transport de bagages et enfin un vaste coffre accessible de l'extérieur. Voiture de sport racée et cabriolet élégant réunis en un seul et même véhicule. Radio, chauffage, dégivreur et ventilation, aménagement luxueux et équipement de qualité supérieure sont les garants d'une conduite agréable et commode. Avec un rapport de démultiplication de 3,77 : 1 du pont arrière, cette voiture réalise sans peine 150 km/h et fournit des accélérations extraordinaires.

Graber's variations on the Alvis theme had a purity of line and cleverly utilized the Alvis radiator, though the Sport Special was less effective without it.

ALVIS 3 litres Coupé carrossé par

Spécialement destinée aux connaisseurs, l'ALVIS 3 litres est une voiture qui transforme la simple conduite en un véritable plaisir. La qualité propre de l'ALVIS est mise particulièrement en évidence sur ce modèle, dont l'aménagement intérieur témoigne par son raffinement de la sûreté de goût de ses créateurs. Les instruments, l'indicateur de vitesse et le poste de radio sont disposés de manière claire et aisément accessible dans un tableau de bord en bois précieux. Les sièges antérieurs sont séparés et facilement réglables. Le coffre à bagages est très largement dimensionné; la roue de secours est logée sur un plateau séparé à charnières, permettant de la retirer sans toucher aux bagages. Le moteur de 3 litres à 6 cylindres avec rapport presque carré de la course à l'alésage a été conçu spécialement en vue de l'obtention d'un rendement élevé à bas régime; il se révèle exceptionnellement souple et nerveux. Par l'efficacité de ses freins hydrauliques, par la précision et la douceur de sa direction, par sa tenue de route inégalée, l'ALVIS forme une classe à part et possède une individualité très marquée. Cette voiture est naturellement équipée de l'excellente installation de chauffage, de dégivrage et de ventilation Smith.

The egg-box grille and disc wheels rather spoil the lines of this right-hand-drive but Swiss-registered Graber coupe.

bodies had been imported by Alvis from Switzerland for the purpose, having being given permission by the Board of Trade. They were registered in Coventry as SHP 642 and TDU 810, and bore consecutive chassis numbers 25858 and 25859 – only 40 chassis away from the last TC that Alvis were to produce.

Since they would shortly have nothing left to sell other than Graber's very small production, the ubiquitous Horsfield put forward a plan: it was uneconomic to import completed bodies from Switzerland, which required permits and attracted import duties of 33%, but there was a possibility that the bodies could be manufactured in Britain under licence. Therefore, he sought quotes from Mann Egerton of Norwich and Willowbrook in Loughborough.

Willowbrook was chosen, which was a strange choice since the firm was a bus-builder with no experience of the delicacies involved in producing sporting saloons. However, the firm was experienced in low-volume hand production of vehicles. The firm's chairman and managing director, William Sutton, announced that car-making had come to Loughborough to stay.

The all-in cost of the body was to be £750 and the initial order was for 25 bodies, with more to come if the quality was right. The body series was to be numbered 56001 to 56025, with the first two digits denoting the year of manufacture.

The prototype was expected by February 1956, with deliveries beginning in April. The agreeable Herr Graber was paid 50,000 Swiss francs for the body manufacturing rights of what was to become known rather clumsily as the TC 108G, but the figure bore no relation to either engine output or top speed.

In the meantime, one of the two sample coupes on the Grey Lady chassis appeared at the Paris motor show, where it won instant approval. Nearly 30 orders for British delivery were taken. A few weeks later, when the car appeared at Earls Court, there was further acclaim.

The Autocar talked of Alvis moving away from upright bodywork and producing 'one of the most beautifully-proportioned cars to be displayed at Earls Court'. Apart from the neat, familiar, radiator

grille carrying the red triangle, there was no point of reference to identify it with Alvises of the past, and even the radiator lost its traditional external filler cap.

The thin screen pillars and large glass area gave the appearance of a hardtop coupe, accentuated by the two-door configuration and the partial wraparound of the rear window. The whole impression was of a fast, elegant car with a light and airy interior.

The full-width bodywork concealed clever body engineering. The car had a notable rigidity: the bulkhead was bolted through to plates welded to the chassis on either side of the radiator; deep box-section sills ran the length of the wheelbase; the wings were an integral part of the structure and not, as in the past, separate items bolted through beading to the main shell.

Beneath the new skin lay the orthodox Grey Lady mechanicals, but the car weighed considerably less; a motor show brochure described it as being only 27½cwt (3,080lb) whereas the Grey Lady had put on weight and reached 30¾cwt (3,444lb). At £2,621 it was also considerably more expensive compared with the Grey Lady's £1,821.

A short road test by *The Motor* described it rather curiously as being 'reminiscent of the brief delights of caviare or of schnapps', and reported that it was one of the quietest cars ever driven, with negligible wind and road noise. Roadholding was praised, but there was criticism of the way the plated bezels of the circular instruments reflected in the windscreen and also of that pernicious invention, the umbrella handbrake under the dashboard.

A later *Autocar* test recorded a top speed of 103mph and a 0–60mph figure of 13.5sec, which was 3 seconds faster than the old Grey Lady and, not dismayed by the price hike, the magazine reported that if you had the money, it was hard to think of a better way of spending it.

The *Coventry Evening Telegraph* was ecstatic: 'This truly

magnificent car ... without doubt marks the rebirth of Alvis as car producers.' The car was a clear success, with 100 orders on the books by the beginning of 1956. However, there were still only two demonstration cars in the country and renaissance was some way away. By May, Willowbrook were still waiting to begin work, but the Graber jigs were held up at Customs. Alvis had bought materials for 25 chassis and engines, which were to be built in the service department at Holyhead Road, and there were hopes that British-built Grabers would be ready for the Earls Court show in the autumn.

The jigs, which eventually arrived, were timber formers on which the wings, wheelarches and radiator cowling were shaped in 18-gauge steel. The roof, bonnet and bootlid were similarly fabricated, but in aluminium. The body was built-up and welded on a slave frame before being transferred to the chassis, which had a resin-bonded plywood floor. Almost all this work was done by hand and machine rather than by using pressings – the cost of which had sunk two previous Alvis projects.

One unusual feature was the instrument panel, which was moulded in glassfibre rather than carved from wood, and had large recessed instrument dials.

By October 1956, Willowbrook had managed to complete only three cars, two of which appeared at the motor show, one in silver grey and the other in cream and green. The price had shot up to £3,450, which led to the cancellation of 60 of the orders which had been outstanding since the start of the year, though some new orders were taken at the show after 12 demonstration runs, so that about 30 were left on the books.

Graber at his best; the long, low lines of a Sports convertible, seen here at the Geneva motor show.

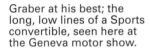

At nearly £3,500 the TC 108G was dearer than the Aston Martin DB2/4 and a few pounds less than the Bristol 405. Since it is difficult to relate the cost to today's prices, it is instructive to note

how much of a luxury car this Alvis was; the same price would buy three new Austin A95 Westminsters with almost enough left over to add an A35.

It was Stanley Horsfield's ever-optimistic view that more Press interest and further advertising would produce a market for 100 cars, which Willowbrook were prepared to build at the rate of two per week, but more caution and even an end to car production was now being urged.

This had been considered at a board meeting just before the motor show. It was a decision, said John Parkes, which 'would be reached only with the greatest reluctance, having regard to the high reputation which the company enjoyed in the motoring world'. The financial director had no such qualms; now that Alvis had reduced its car stocks to negligible proportions the car business should be shut down. It had made heavy losses over the previous five years, which had eaten deeply into the profits of other departments.

Parkes managed to postpone the decision yet again and went to visit Willowbrook to find out why production was delayed. There was a sad tale to hear. Willowbrook's chairman, William Sutton, complained that the few bodies that they had made so far had cost an estimated £2,000 each because of the cost of making panels by hand, whereas Alvis were paying them only £750 each. He wanted an order for another 100 bodies to justify spending £5,000 on panel tools. It was not forthcoming.

Graber himself was becoming impatient as Alvis chassis production had diminished to almost nothing: 'I am sorry that Alvis do not do more for the moment in the motor car department and that it (sic) does not risk more,' he wrote. 'Unfortunately my 1957 programme cannot be fulfilled any more. It was my intention to order at least 20 chassis, which cars I would have sold for certain.'

In the meantime, there was more woe at Willowbrook. Sutton

halved his estimate of what the Alvis bodies were costing him to £1,100, but said he needed an order of between 200 and 250 rather than 25 because his finances could not withstand the loss. Haggling ensued, and Sutton offered to make 100 bodies at £850 if Alvis paid £6,000 for tools. By this time it was obvious that Willowbrook were not going to be able to deliver even the original order, and Alvis cast around for other suppliers.

A body was sent for an estimate to Boulton and Paul, the aircraft manufacturers. They quoted £350 unfinished, which Willowbrook

This convertible, which is badged TC 108G at the rear, was built in Switzerland and exhibited at the 1957 Earls Court show.

The dash of the same car, revealing its typical Continental style.

then wanted another £500 to finish. Jensen in West Bromwich suggested £300 per body. It was all very unsatisfactory. By March 1957, nearly 18 months after the TC 108G had first appeared in Britain, only eight Willowbrook cars had been sold. Three more were in production and one was waiting to be sold at Brooklands, in London. There had been slight changes from the Graber original. The steering column became adjustable and more legroom was found for rear seat passengers, partly by moving the rear squab back 2 inches. There were also minor changes in switch positions. Development work continued with revised pedal arrangements, effected by moving the toeboard and pedals forward 2in, and experimentation with a new BMC gearbox from the Austin-Healey to replace the Alvis version, which dated back to the 12/70. It was first tried by Hermann Graber on his personal TC 21/100.

By June deliveries had improved, with 11 cars being sold and one supplied on sale-or-return to Brooklands. The sales department did some elementary market research by contacting the first eight buyers. They were all reported to be very satisfied with the car, giving appearance, individuality, reliability, roadholding and performance as a fast touring vehicle as reasons for buying it.

However, the distributors were more gloomy. The sales manager reported: 'There is a certain amount of apathy towards Alvis, as the general impression is that either we are going out of the motor car industry, or in one or two cases that we have already gone out.'

Demonstrations were few, and those prospective buyers who did take a test drive were put off by the price and the fear that the company would go out of business. The main competitors were identified as Lagonda, Bristol, Aston Martin and the Jaguar 2.4 and 3.4 saloons.

By the time of the 1957 autumn motor shows, Alvis had the embarrassment of exhibiting cars for which they could give no

The Willowbrook-built cars copied the same basic design, though the reflective instrument bezels were not liked.

The elegance of Graber's style is well portrayed in this shot of a drophead coupe, although the white-wall tyres are an unusual touch.

delivery dates, so no orders were taken. The Graber-styled and built drophead coupe appeared for the first time, with its neat head which folded right down into the body sides and a recess behind the rear seat squab; it was covered by a tonneau secured by press-studs.

It was priced the same as for the saloon at £3,450, and according to Alvis salesmen on the stand, while the public made no comment about the prices, the distributors called for a cut to under £3,000. Despite the paucity of models, the cars were enthusiastically received. 'The Three-litre has a lively performance and is ideally suited to fast long-distance Continental touring,' said *The Autocar*. 'The interior furnishings reach luxury standards and the car is excellently finished.'

The Alvis strategy was that those cars which could be produced for the British market would be made in Loughborough and Coventry, while cars for export would be made by Graber in Switzerland. At the 1958 Geneva show in March, Graber displayed the TC 108G and two versions of his own: the smaller, lighter Special coupe and the mildly-tuned Super. They looked rather different from the standard models, with a new radiator grille with a centre strip, and different treatment of the bonnet and rear roof section. The Coventry cars also had a change in the rear roof section, which was raised and extended to give more room to passengers.

Apart from the few chassis made for Graber and Willowbrook, Alvis had produced almost no cars for quite a while, yet at about this time they considered a move into mass-production with, of all

This is one of the rare Willowbrook cars, registered DEK 385, which was built in 1957 on chassis number 25928.

things, the Isetta bubble car, in which they were prepared to pour substantial sums. The idea, which is perhaps kindly described as quixotic, was to produce 600 of the BMW-designed Isettas, mainly for export. However, the sudden drop in popularity of bubble cars when petrol rationing ended with the resolution of the Suez crisis left hundreds unsold, particularly in Canada, and the project was abandoned at some considerable cost.

Another lost cause was the Willowbrook contract as production stopped after some 15 or 16 TC 108G bodies were built. Fourteen bodies that were put on to chassis have been traced, though there could have been one more complete car, and in addition there was one unmounted body.

Willowbrook were subsequently taken over by the Duple coachbuilding firm, and while the cars which were produced have a rarity value, the build quality, despite the handwork involved, is not as good as those cars which were to follow. A particularly weak point was the wooden front door posts, which were too small for the weight of the doors.

Twenty-two Graber versions of the TC 108G were completed, with some in cabriolet form. By the end of 1957 the value of the Alvis order book stood at:

	£
CARS	9,000
AERO-ENGINES	495,000
FIGHTING VEHICLES	745,000
SUNDRIES	58,000

The car manufacturer had become a defence contractor. Yet, in many ways, the best was yet to come to fulfil the original automotive ambitions of T G John.

15

PARK WARD
AND THE TD 21

Now that the Willowbrook contract had ended in recrimination and arguments about money, it was essential to find yet another coachbuilder if Alvis were to stay in production.

Park Ward in North London, who had been taken over by Rolls-Royce in 1947, had a very high reputation for their work on Bentley and Rolls, and it was to them that Alvis next turned for the successor to the TC 108G. The result was the TD 21, a revised body on the familiar engine and chassis which had begun with the TA 21. Park Ward also guaranteed that they could make the bodies cheaper than Willowbrook.

At the beginning of 1958 a chassis was sent to the Park Ward works at 473 High Road, Willesden, for tooling examinations; this was probably the first Park Ward prototype, car number 25938, later registered 9 VMG. Graber, who was receiving a licence fee for his design, came to Britain to discuss the prototype.

It was based on a Graber design of about 1956, which he himself had abandoned on his own coachbuilt cars in favour of a new lower line, with a wide curved grille. Graber's royalties from Alvis were calculated not on each car sold, but only on each drophead, with the sum being credited to his account against his purchase of chassis.

Further work was continuing in the experimental department in Coventry which involved fitment of the BMC gearbox from the Austin-Healey and the development of new pedal arrangements, by which the pedals were to be put a further 3 inches forward; modifications were made to the brake and clutch master cylinders to lower the front floor.

Meanwhile, Park Ward had begun drawing some preliminary designs for treatment of the rear, which included more space again for the rear seat passengers and the provision of space in the boot for two sets of golf clubs, which was not possible in the Willowbrook cars.

There was also a change in the frontal area; one drawing from February 1958 shows spotlights recessed into the front wings, which is a feature that did not appear until the Mark 2 model a year later. Park Ward further proposed to install the same 3.5kW heating system as they were fitting into the Bentley.

A preliminary arrangement was signed in January for Park Ward to produce 25 pre-production cars before the end of 1958, of which

at least 12 were to be ready by the autumn London motor show. Regular production was to start in January 1959, with an output of five cars per week by the spring of that year. A formal contract followed to produce 1,000 bodies at a cost of £750 for the saloon and £800 for the coupe. Graber agreed to import the completed cars to sell in Switzerland, but would continue to manufacture his Special saloon and coupe bodies at his own works in Berne. He was continuing to be successful with them; at the Geneva show in March 1958 he sold four cars off the stand and said he could have sold another eight.

Willowbrook had made the bodies almost entirely by hand, beating the panels to shape over wooden formers. Park Ward, whose production until then was no more than two cars a week, went a stage further. While neither they nor Alvis could afford mass-production press tools for all the body panels, they adopted a half-way solution of mechanization by using a rubber press and a stretch press. The rubber press worked by forming the panel over a die using the pressure of thick blocks of rubber; the stretch press, a 300-ton hydraulic Erco, stretched the material to shape.

Other parts, like the floor, were manufactured without any pressings and were built up from flat sheet steel using the new technology of spot-welding. Another novelty was the part-use of plastic filler rather than 100% lead-loading to mask imperfections. The roof, bonnet and bootlid were aluminium.

The Autocar, reporting on the production process, said that all assemblies were jig-built to ensure accuracy, then the three main assemblies were tested against an Alvis master chassis. There followed many coats of filler and stopper before the six coats of colour. Many of the components such as the wiring harness were then fitted to the body before it joined the chassis as a completed car. Transporters then took the completed cars back to Coventry for final road-testing and despatch to the dealers.

Alvis announced to the Press early in 1958 that a new car was on the way. Production plans were said to be made for a considerable number of models, with a large price reduction over the TC 108G. At Holyhead Road, new equipment was installed in No 1 machine shop to deal with the resumption of major chassis production, and slowly the facelifted model began to take shape. Inquiries flooded

Park Ward's frontal drawings for the new Alvis in February 1958. Though the TD 21 went into production with rectangular air vents each side of the radiator, a variation of the recessed-lamp style was adopted for the Series II.

The car carrying the registration number 9 VMG was the first chassis sent to Park Ward and was used by them extensively to test body styling. Its appearance now, with a front similar to the TD Series II and a dash like the TF, is likely to be quite different from its 1958 shape.

in and there was keen expectation as to what would appear at Earls Court.

Almost every inquirer wanted to know whether disc brakes would be fitted; this caused some anxiety at the factory as the plan was to offer the car with the same Lockheed twin-leading-shoe drum brakes; it was eventually decided to offer servo-assisted Lockheed discs on the front as a £15 option until all the cars with drum brakes had been sold, though none appears to have been fitted on the early cars. Many cars were subsequently modified with discs at the works during services.

Other mechanical changes were Lockheed hydraulic operation of the Borg and Beck clutch and an improved mounting for the radiator. Borg-Warner automatic transmission was an optional extra.

The new car was first shown to the Press in early September 1958, and only those with a close knowledge of Alvis would have noted the difference between it and its predecessor. Most obvious, perhaps, was the rear window profile which was now one piece of glass rather than three, with less wraparound. The rear wing line was slightly higher, the rear light clusters changed and bumpers were of different section, with the number-plate at the rear removed from the bumper and inserted in a recessed section in the back panel with reversing lamps. Much was made of the size of the boot,

Body panels being assembled on the jig at Park Ward's factory in north west London.

which was now large enough to accommodate the marketing department's requirement of two sets of golf clubs, although this was achieved at the expense of rear body rigidity.

At the front, the distinguishing change was two small horizontal grilles in the nose below the headlamps, utilized to duct air from the right-hand grille to the heater and from the left-hand one to the two flat AC filters on the SU carburettors, so aiding the breathing problems which had afflicted earlier Three-litres. There were also separate miniature sidelights.

The major changes occurred inside and were made in response to complaints about lack of room in the rear. Headroom was increased by 3 inches and legroom was improved by dropping the floor slightly; the work of moving the pedals forward also helped by moving the relative position of the front seats. It was notable that although only a two-door car, rear passengers could get in and out without tipping forward the front seats, as a result of 42.5in wide doors. However, these were to bring their own problems. The rear end, whilst now providing more room, was more boxy in shape and some of Graber's original curvature was lost.

The moulded glassfibre dash of the earlier model was replaced by a much more traditional walnut veneer panel in the centre of the car carrying a speedometer next to the driver, a rev-counter, ancillary instruments and sliding heater controls. It was a great improvement on the previous painted layout and would have pleased the pilot in John Parkes, an ex-de Havilland man, since it resembled the binnacle of a small plane.

The saloon had a headlining of cream or grey Vynide rather than cloth, which had been criticized for picking up dust. The drophead coupe had a hood of Everflex, which was available in six different colours and lined with beige or grey West of England cloth, and this, of course, retracted into the car sides, so reducing the rear seat width from 49.5 to 43in. Seating was luxurious, made of Connolly Vaumol hide, and was available in seven different shades: tan, red, off-white, pale blue, green, grey and Alvis brick red. The door sills and pillars were covered with polished 'super purity' aluminium.

As for paintwork, owners could specify whatever they wanted at extra charge; for instance, two-tone non-factory paint was about £50 extra. However, there was plenty of choice in the standard range, with eight colours available: Alice blue, midnight blue, mist green, Alvis standard light grey, Alvis standard seal grey, silver grey 5331, peony and black.

The Park Ward car was slightly lighter in weight than its predecessor, but many pounds cheaper. At the 1957 London show the saloon was £3,451; by the 1958 show it had dropped to £2,993 (a pound for every cc!), with the coupe priced at £3,293. Extras were a Smith's Radiomobile 200RB at £48 and the Borg-Warner automatic gearbox at £134. The heater by now was standard.

So after two years in which virtually no cars were produced, Alvis were back in business as a car maker. Distributors from all over Britain were invited to the factory over a period of three days and they liked what they saw. At Earls Court arrangements were made for selling to Canada, where the agents were to be the Rolls-Royce distributors in Toronto and Vancouver.

When the show ended, two demonstration cars were on the road

The hood mechanism of a drophead coupe being installed at Park Ward.

constantly in Britain, and by December 77 orders had been received since the car had been announced. However, all was not well since some orders had been lost due to the BMC gearbox. Two different versions were fitted, the BN4 and the BN7, differing only in their ratios.

Distributors and customers complained that it was difficult to engage first and reverse gears without synchromesh, and that it was noisy in the intermediate gears. The engineering view was that the gearbox could not really cope with the torque of the Alvis engine, though it may well have been perfectly suitable for BMC cars. The sales director admitted that the gearbox was not acceptable and pinned his hopes on more customers buying the optional Borg-Warner automatic. Nevertheless, the TD 21 had a deservedly warm welcome as an elegant, luxurious 100mph car, and was a worthy bearer of the famous red triangle. *The Motor* even went so far as to describe it as having a 'Jeeves-like quality of responding to its master's whim'.

There seems to have been no proper road test of this revised version until a major change in February 1959, when a long-awaited modification was made by installing a new cylinder head. The engine had been in production for nearly a decade, and as previously noted, its designer Chris Kingham had wanted to put an overhead-cam cylinder head on it some years before, but the

Nearing the end of the production line. At the rear of the picture a chassis and body are about to come together. On the right are a Rolls-Royce Silver Cloud and a Bentley Continental. The trim shop is at the rear.

A Series I comes back from Park Ward for final testing at Holyhead Road.

TD chassis frames piled outside the rear of the works in 1959.

A photograph of a very early TD facia taken for a brochure.

development money had gone into an aero-engine.

The new head, which was an adaptation of the pushrod unit, was designed to perform two functions: to increase power by 20%, and to avoid the Achilles heel of the Three-litre – cracking between the valve seats due to overheating.

An Alvis engineering note of February 1959, detailing the changes, records the admission that the heat-path around the exhaust valve was rather long on one side. Therefore the exhaust port was altered to allow an even thickness of metal in the water-jacketing around the valve seat. A change in water distribution was also implemented with the deletion of copper tube in the head.

The other major engineering change was the provision of six separate ports, one for each valve; previously siamesed inlets were used for cylinders one and two and cylinders five and six. The valves were also slightly offset to give better combustion, which led to the pushrods being inclined outwards at the top. As a result of these streamlining changes, the compression ratio went up from 8:1 to 8.5:1, taking advantage of the availability of higher-octane fuel.

A TD Series I saloon carrying the familiar number XDU 472, which identifies it as the car tested by *The Autocar* early in 1960.

Larger carburettors – two of the new SU HD6 type – replaced the HD4s and Purolator micronic air filters were used to silence intake roar. The single carburettor of the early engine, having become two, was eventually to become three on the TF, for tests at this stage had

One of the first drophead coupes, showing commendable ease of access to the rear seats.

Yes, it will all fit in. Golf clubs figured regularly in brochures as the earlier Willowbrook cars had been much criticized for not accommodating them.

The rear number-plate panel of this Series I was replaced by a neater design in the subsequent model.

already shown that even with two carburettors, feeding three cylinders each, there was a tendency for the incoming air/petrol mixture to be distributed unevenly. Breathing was much improved when each instrument fed only two ports.

There seems to be some dispute as to exactly how much extra power the new six-port head provided. Alvis claimed a 20% increase from the previous engine's 104bhp at 4,200rpm without specifying the maximum. *The Motor* claimed the maximum was 120bhp at 5,000rpm, although *The Autocar* later stated it to be 115bhp at 4,000rpm. Indeed, comparing the *Autocar* test of the first imported Graber saloon in March 1957 with its test of the TD 21 in October 1959, there is virtually no difference in performance figures, although the TD 21 was 140lb heavier.

The increase in power was attained without compromising the original design specification laid down 10 years previously for an engine with refined running and good torque at low and medium speeds as the improvements brought about by the changes were mainly to be seen at crankshaft speeds above 3,000rpm.

Minor engineering changes included a revised water pump to try to abolish overheating permanently and an external replaceable filter for the oil rather than the gauze strainer floating in the sump.

The process of revising the model was important, but subsequent improvements were to take much longer to implement.

16

PROBLEMS AT PARK WARD

Cars with the revised engine appeared first at the Geneva motor show in March 1959. Alvis exhibited a Park Ward saloon and a drophead, while Graber had two Special bodies on his own stand. Much to the chagrin of the men from Coventry, Graber sold four cars and Alvis none. There were mutterings back at Holyhead Road that he should try harder to sell the Park Ward cars which he was importing, possibly by reducing his prices and his profits.

By May of that year, Alvis had built and sold more than 60 TD 21s, of which almost two-thirds were fitted with the optional Borg-Warner automatic transmission. There were nearly 100 orders outstanding, and although Park Ward production was up to seven bodies a week, waiting times were still lengthening. It was a three-month wait for a saloon and three and a half for the drophead; orders were being lost as a result, and Park Ward was asked to increase production from six or seven bodies a week to 10.

By July 110 cars had been sold, but there was a lengthening delay on the delivery of coupe bodies, and some of the hard-won Canadian orders were delayed. Nevertheless, chassis production was maintained and there was talk of taking on more staff at the works in Holyhead Road to cope with demand, which was steady and increasing.

At the Earls Court show in 1959, the distributors made it clear that they wanted changes to freshen the car's appeal. They asked for a new frontal treatment, improved bumpers with more wraparound, modifications to the rear number-plate lighting and the dashboard to be moved from the centre of the car to a position in front of the driver. On the mechanical side, they asked for more power low down in the range and disc brakes to be added all round. The response was slow, to say the least, since most of the changes took years to incorporate, though one change for the 1960 model year was the option of overdrive.

There were also other, more pressing problems to address. Complaints were coming in of poor workmanship at Park Ward. The first manifestations were of water leaks and the doors dropping: 'We have run into a great deal of trouble with the coachwork,' said a report to the Alvis board. Strong protests were made to Park Ward, who despatched representatives to dealers to try to fix the problems. While they were able to make modifications to stop the leaks, they could not prevent the doors jamming. This structural defect was caused by the very large, ash-framed, heavy steel doors, which put an unacceptable strain on the wooden A-post. The difficulties were ameliorated to some extent by the almost total lack of complaints on the mechanical side.

By January 1960, with more than 150 cars sold, the body problems had reached what was called 'an alarming stage'. The sales manager reported that the majority of Park Ward cars had jamming doors, including some with under 1,000 miles on the clock. Customers were objecting to having their doors adjusted three or four times with no apparent effect, and some distributors were refusing to take any more cars until the defect was eliminated. There were even fears that dealers would abandon Alvis altogether.

An Alvis deputation comprising the chairman, works director, chief engineer and service manager descended on Willesden and were told by Park Ward that a chassis weakness was responsible. This they strongly disputed, but agreed to strengthen the chassis and to strip a car for examination.

An *Autocar* road test in October 1959 on XVC 534 had said: 'Park Ward build high-quality coachwork to last – at a price.' Mike Dunn, who was Alvis' chief engineer in the Sixties, believed that the Alvis bodies were built *down* to a price; they did not have the same standards which Park Ward were putting into their Rolls-Royces and Bentleys. The same test, which did not uncover the door problem, disclosed that for added accuracy the doors were hung first and then panelled; it described them as closing with a majestic clunk – more like an air of finality than a noise.

Four months later, when the same magazine tested XDU 472, which had the new engine installed, it found the water leaks which other owners were protesting about, but again had no problems with the doors other than draughts blowing up inside them, and

Works demonstrator 8279 RW, showing the improved rear lower panel on the Series II. The number-plate lamps are in the rear valance.

remarking that they were so wide that in traffic and in a garage they could not be opened far enough.

By March 1960, the quality at Park Ward as far as paintwork and finish were concerned had improved, and two were sold from the Alvis stand at the Geneva show, though Graber himself sold six of his own creations. The ultimate solution to the door problem was some way away; it would be another year before Park Ward came up with modification kits for these and the water leaks − problems which were still making the dealers restive. Many cars were subsequently modified with alloy door panels being substituted for steel in order to reduce weight.

An external factor became more worrying; the Budget imposed a severe credit squeeze. It had always been the intention to build 1,000 chassis for the Park Ward cars and to make them in batches to meet demand. By the time of the 1960 Budget, 232 saloons and 75 coupes had been built and there were orders outstanding for 137 more cars. However, the credit squeeze forced postponement of the next scheduled batch of 100 chassis as orders plunged. The Alvis sales manager reported that not only was there a huge drop in secondhand car prices, but there were large unsold stocks of competitors like the Jaguar Mark IX, and Daimler were offering immediate delivery of their Majestic in any colour.

The Alvis, of course, was never a cheap car to buy, or to run. It was fifth from bottom in an October 1960 *Motor* table of miles per pound of petrol purchased. With a touring consumption of 20.2mpg, £1 worth of petrol at 4s 10d a gallon gave 84 miles.

Because of the general depression, production at Park Ward was cut from 10 to seven cars a week which, the sales manager remarked wryly, should give them the opportunity to improve the finish 'which is even now not up to the standard for a £3,000 car', and was thought to be affecting orders.

The TD engine. The rather crude spark plug shield replaced a much more pleasing alloy cover on earlier Three-litres. By this time, the engine had gained an exterior oil filter.

A chassis being wheeled out of the factory. Note the steady bar to hold the steering column in transit to Park Ward.

It was decided to make no changes for the autumn Earls Court show, which was welcomed for once by the dealers who had unsold stocks to clear. The London distributors, for instance, had received only three orders in two months.

By September, some 430 cars had been completed and change was being thought about, even if not implemented. The original intention was to facelift the car from the 601st TD, introducing, among other things, Dunlop disc brakes all round and a centre armrest at the rear, so that the new car could be shown at Geneva in the spring of 1961, but production difficulties and slow sales postponed this for another year.

The new plan was to clear 750 cars by the Earls Court show in 1961 so that only the revised models would be on sale from then onwards, but again production delays at Park Ward meant that the new TD 21 Series II model was eventually offered alongside existing stocks of the previous model.

The Series II – thought by many to be the most attractive of the Park Ward cars – was announced in April 1962, at a time when the Alvis car division was on a three-day week and Park Ward body production had been halved to 2.5 units a week.

The car incorporated some of the changes for which dealers had been pressing, though it has to be said that they were minor and almost all cosmetic.

The front was given a more pleasing appearance by replacing the horizontal air intake grilles with circular apertures into which the twin foglamps were recessed, but enough space was left around them to allow air through to feed the heater from one side and the carburettors from the other.

At the rear the tail panel below the boot, which had been recessed to contain the number-plate, was smoothed out and the Lucas 469 combined number-plate/reversing light – a dated hangover from the TA 21 – was replaced by separate lamps, with the reversing lights at the side and the number-plate lights in the rear valance.

Mechanically, the only significant change was the scheduled fitting of servo-assisted Dunlop disc brakes front and rear, giving 487sq in of rubbed area compared with 397sq in provided in the Series I Lockheed disc/drum configuration.

The cost of the revised car went up by £100 on the basic price, putting the saloon at £2,881 including tax and the coupe at £3,156. They had to be sold alongside uncleared stocks of the Series I, still at its old price, which took more than a year to shift.

By this time the wooden door-pillar problems had been solved. The in-joke among Alvis aficionados was they did not mind wood as part of the structure of the car, as long as the tree had stopped growing! The wooden pillars were resin-bonded and to achieve greater lightness the door frames were now constructed of aluminium, as were the panels.

Later in 1962 came the significant improvement of the introduction, at no extra cost, of a manual five-speed gearbox from the German company of Zahnradfabrik, Friedrichshafen. The four lower ZF ratios were the same as in the four-speed gearbox, with the fifth gear being a step-up ratio similar to overdrive. With the engine at 1,000rpm it gave 25mph compared with 26mph for the overdrive on the previous unit. The Borg-Warner automatic transmission was still available as a £130 option.

Because the original BMC gearbox was unsatisfactory, many owners had specified automatic transmission. An *Autocar* test in August 1962 of 8192 RW showed that it was only 2mph slower, at 101.5mph, than the manual car. From 0–60mph it took 16.6sec, which was 3 seconds slower than the manual. The testers were impressed with the car, which now weighed 31.25cwt (3,500lb), except for a slow take-up into first gear on kick-down, which caused the engine to overspeed.

The Borg-Warner gearbox had a variable intermediate hold control, which meant that in 'minimum' the car started in intermediate gear unless the accelerator was kicked down, while in 'maximum' it started in low and changed up at 24 and 53mph.

The ZF gearbox and other changes went down well at the Earls Court show in 1962, which was the fourth year the TD 21 had been seen there, but the usual crop of complaints ensued from the dealers and public. By this time more than 800 TD 21 models had been sold, and despite gradual changes, there were calls for yet further improvements, possibly because of the progress which other manufacturers were making.

The complaints centred mainly on the steering, which was admittedly heavy, but at this stage no power assistance was envisaged. The sales manager believed that the lack of power-steering as an option was the greatest cause of sales resistance. There were also adverse comments about the steering lock given by the Burman box. Three and three-quarter turns from lock-to-lock gave a turning circle between kerbs of some 41ft 9in to the right and 42ft 7in to the left. Harsh suspension at the front was also mentioned.

The dealers also wanted more cosmetic alteration; their view was that the TD Series I and II were practically indistinguishable externally, which made it difficult to persuade Alvis owners to change.

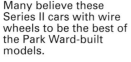

Many believe these Series II cars with wire wheels to be the best of the Park Ward-built models.

There were, however, other matters on the minds of the Alvis board. In December 1962 – by which time 650 TD saloons and 200 coupes had been delivered – a strange item appeared in *The Motor*: 'Alvis Ltd have announced their intention to maintain production of their saloon and coupe models during 1963.' It was an announcement of the obvious which must have surprised many owners. The basis for it may well have been that word had leaked out of further secret discussions between John Parkes, for Alvis, and the David Brown Corporation, makers, among other things, of Aston Martin and Lagonda cars. The association between Lagonda and Alvis went back some time. Alvis bid for the firm unsuccessfully in 1935 and after the war was said to have been offered Lagonda for £75,000, although there is no record of the offer in the Alvis board papers.

The new approach was a proposal for pooling resources. The plan was for Alvis to take over manufacture of the six-cylinder 3,670cc engine for the Aston Martin DB4 and to make commercial gearboxes for David Brown.

In early 1963, further proposals came from David Brown which included a joint company to run car sales and distribution. The directors at Holyhead Road were not at all sure about this and insisted that the name Alvis be kept.

Further suggestions were the adaptation of the 4-litre Lagonda version of the DB4 engine for the TD, and for the manufacture by Alvis of 500 Aston Martin engines and chassis per year at a cost below that at which David Brown could make them, though Aston would make the same number. Aston's general manager, John Wyer, revealed later that the joint venture of 1,000 units per year would have had Aston concentrating on performance and Alvis on the luxury side of the market. Alvis were given Sir David Brown's personal DB4 for a month when he received his next factory car.

The Alvis experimental department had some thought of re-engining the Three-litre; on one occasion at Holyhead Road there was a Park Ward car with a locked bonnet under which could be found the triple twin-choke Solex-equipped Lagonda engine. The bonnet was locked because there was no room for the conventional centre bonnet lock. Alvis had the car for about 11 months; Mike Dunn, who drove it a great deal, remembered it as a super car, though it had only a four-speed gearbox. He recorded an indicated 135mph on the MIRA test track.

However, the discussions came to nothing and the project ended. Alvis removed the Lagonda engine, but Aston seemed to have forgotten about it, so Dunn sent it back to them some 18 months later.

John Wyer was quoted as saying that one of the reasons for the project's failure was that the re-engined Alvis would have competed directly against the Lagonda Rapide, which Sir David Brown would not countenance, though Sir David himself thinks this was not the case.

Apart from any conflict over Lagonda, the Alvis board decided themselves not to pursue matters as the David Brown Corporation were frequently changing their minds about their requirements. So, for the second time in 10 years, the Alvis/Aston Martin Lagonda project ended in failure.

17

SERIES III – THE TE 21

In Alvis' confusing nomenclature, the long-awaited facelift of the TD was known as the Three-litre Series III, or the TE 21; while the production side wanted to call it simply TE 21, the sales department insisted upon adding the Series III. The car was announced for the Earls Court show in October 1963 and the front looked dramatically different from the TD as it had twin-stacked headlights.

This idea had come from Graber's display at the Geneva show in the spring, when he showed a four-door saloon on the Alvis chassis in addition to his Special and Super. All the exhibits had stacked headlights, an arrangement reminiscent of the Mercedes of the time, although a similar idea had also been adopted, using a slightly different alignment, for the Rolls-Royce Silver Cloud 'Chinese eye' model. According to some, though, the car that the Alvis resembled most closely was the Facel Vega.

Some consideration was given in Coventry to adopting the four-door saloon, but it was decided that the costs would be too great. However, the vertical two-headlight style was adopted, using the new Lucas sealed-beam units of 5.75in diameter mounted in a plated surround. Mike Dunn, who was then chief engineer, said that Parkes had insisted on it, even though most people at Holyhead Road hated the style.

The lower headlight replaced the faired-in driving lamps and horizontal grilles appeared again as air intakes for carburettors and heater. The change also gave a higher wing line at the front, which was not to everyone's taste, and at the rear there was a minor reshaping of the wings. Wire wheels were offered at an extra cost of £30.

Dunn was given his head to make the other alterations, resulting in yet more power being squeezed out of Chris Kingham's 1950 engine, which originally put out 86bhp. It now produced 130bhp at 5,000rpm, with torque increased from the 156lb.ft of the TD to 172lb.ft at 3,250rpm. This was achieved by increases of 2mm in the diameter of both the inlet and exhaust valves, stronger valve springs and alterations in the exhaust manifolds and piping. New KA needles were fitted to the twin SU carburettors to improve economy, but what effect they had was doubtful. The exhaust system back pressure was reduced by new silencers and larger diameter pipes of 1.75in.

However, considerable warranty problems were caused by the

additional power which was now available; the engine had been designed before the days of motorways, and over-enthusiastic drivers tended to go through crankshafts at an alarming rate. A service 'fix' by dealers required the distributor vacuum advance pipe to be blanked off, thus cutting back the advance curve. While this lengthened engine life, it also reduced brake horsepower.

Other mechanical modifications included changes to the steering box, fitting ball bearings in the idler lever assembly, to answer criticisms of heavy steering, and the fitting of a Borg and Beck 9.5in diameter diaphragm clutch.

John Parkes had always been interested in ergonomics and he suggested several changes to the grouping of the minor controls on the dash; for instance, he wanted the panel dimmer switch to be next to the ignition switch so that he could find it easily to switch it off at night as his pilot's training had taught him. Ashtrays were moved from the doors to the facia. The spare-wheel tray – always a trial to lift and lower – had over-centre levers fitted to make the operation easier.

The cost of the car went up by £200 on the basic price to a tax-paid £2,773 for the saloon and £3,015 for the coupe, though direct comparisons with previous prices are not relevant because of the large number of changes in purchase tax.

The modifications were again welcomed at Earls Court, but there was continuing pressure for power-steering, despite the changes made to the Burman gearbox. By February 1964, only 10 orders had been taken since the show. Alvis blamed Park Ward as they were now quoting three months' delivery for saloons and five for coupes.

The manufacture of cars had become a sideline for Alvis, but

Graber's stacked-headlight idiom, which took the fancy of Alvis chairman John Parkes, was demonstrated on this car in Geneva.

The stacked headlights significantly altered both the frontal appearance and the wing line of the TE 21 compared with earlier cars in the series.

Parkes was still determined to continue for prestige reasons, and although there were not many chassis left to complete the requirement of 1,000 he began again to cast around for body suppliers.

There were discussions with their neighbour, Carbodies, who might have been in a position to build the four-door saloon, but these talks ended abruptly after Parkes had crossed the road to their works. He said the work he had seen there was not up to Alvis standards. One of the Alvis directors, who was also chairman of Scottish Aviation, offered to build the bodies in his own works, but finally it was decided to stick with Park Ward, and another 100 bodies were ordered to be delivered at the rate of four a week.

Orders trickled in during 1964 until the motor show, when suddenly 27 orders were taken in five weeks – 23 of them for cars with the new power-steering, which at long last had been introduced. Had Alvis responded earlier to the insistent calls for this feature, orders might well have been brisker.

Like the gearbox, the power-steering came from ZF in Germany. It was a recirculating-ball unit, used for the first time on a British car, whose pump was driven off the end of the dynamo. The effect, of course, was to reduce heaviness, but it also reduced the steering turns lock-to-lock from three and a third to two and three quarters.

The new option cost £120 and, according to *The Motor*, was well worth having. An *Autocar* road test in April 1965 of ARW 899B agreed; it called the steering pleasantly light, which meant that 'a woman can now manoeuvre and park easily'.

This was the time when car magazines began to make criticisms of the cars they tested rather than lavishing unstinting praise,

though *The Autocar* could find only two problems with the TE. One was a thumping sound when driving over joints or ridges in the road, which was due to the lack of fore-and-aft compliance in the suspension, a solution to which had only recently been discovered by other car manufacturers. The other problem was a clicking noise when selecting gear. *The Autocar* helpfully suggested that nylon rather than steel balls should be used in the ZF gearbox.

The magazine was also unsure about the double headlights; the main beams were less penetrating for fast night driving, but on dip there was better illumination.

Performance figures with the uprated engine were given as 12.5sec from 0–60mph, with a top speed of 108mph, and there was praise for the car's ability to cruise effortlessly at 100mph. However, the overall fuel consumption of 15.9mpg was disappointing and untypical as 20mph was obtained regularly in factory tests.

The verdict, as in most of the postwar tests, was that the Alvis character was maintained by combining pleasing qualities of the past with desirable features of the moment.

Several TD cars were later uprated with the TE mechanicals, the most notable being the Series I drophead coupe owned by the Duke of Edinburgh. The car, registered with his personal prefix OXR 1 (the Queen's is MYT; say it quickly!), was chassis number 26600, halfway through the TD sequence. It was delivered in June 1961 with standard mechanicals and overdrive, but there were some changes to the bodywork. The windscreen was made taller because of his height, which gave the car a higher roofline, and the dashboard was, like in the song, genuine leather.

There are tales that there was an uproar when the TE was announced. *The Daily Express* motoring man declared: 'I have a shock for Prince Philip this morning. His £3,000 Alvis drophead coupe is out of date from today. To make things even worse, that model in the royal garage has only two headlights, and the new version has four.' Seasoned readers of the tabloids will detect a certain contrivance here, but despite 'an Alvis executive' being quoted as saying that the royal car could not be adapted, and that if the Prince wanted to bring himself up to date he would have to buy a new TE, a discreet accommodation was made. The car went back to the factory to be fitted with the TE cylinder head and the ZF five-speed box. Who paid? Who knows? The car is now in the museum on the Sandringham estate.

Gracious living portrayed by Alvis and architecture, though more of the former would have been appreciated.

The TE was almost the final flowering of the Alvis era, which began to draw to an end in May 1965. This was when John Parkes made an approach to the Rover chairman, George Farmer, suggesting that an amalgamation of the two companies would be in their best interests.

It must have been a difficult decision to renounce the independence of Alvis after more than 40 years, but the economics were remorseless. Alvis by itself was too small and consequently not very successful. Profits after tax of £269,000 in 1960 had declined slightly to £260,000 in 1961 and then fallen more depressingly to £243,000, £206,000 and £142,000 in successive years to 1964. The profits for 1965 were likely to be even less. The vagaries of contracts from the defence industry, on which it was almost wholly dependent, had let Alvis down and there was no salvation from car manufacture, which was now just a tiny part of the business.

On June 2, 1965 George Farmer sent a handwritten note to John Parkes formally offering what he called an amalgamation with Rover, offering one Rover 5 shilling (25p) share for every Alvis ordinary share of the same value and £1 14s (£1.70) in cash for every Alvis £1 preference share. The Alvis board speedily accepted the deal and recommended its acceptance to shareholders, pointing out that both companies manufactured cross-country vehicles and 'high-quality passenger cars'.

In fact it was not an amalgamation, but a takeover by Rover, which was a much larger and much more successful company; Rover's profits the previous year had been 10 times those of Alvis. Despite well-meant Rover protestations that the red triangle would continue to appear on cars from Holyhead Road, it sounded the death knell for the Alvis car.

18

TF 21 – LAST
OF THE LINE

The last model of the Alvis, the so-called Series IV, more commonly known as the TF 21 and now being produced under the Rover aegis, first appeared at the Geneva show in March 1966. There had been some disappointment at the previous Earls Court show that there had been no modifications to the TE 21, which was now two years old.

Production began with car number 27370, a chassis delivered to Graber, as was number 27371. The first Park Ward car was a drophead coupe, number 27372. Just over 100 cars were made because by this time production was trickling towards a standstill as the new owners, Rover, considered a new generation of Alvis cars. Prototype plans were sent to Alvis in the spring of 1966 as, meanwhile, the remainder of the 1,000 or so chassis first authorized for the Park Ward cars needed to be completed.

The TF 21 differed from its predecessor in its internals, becoming the fastest and most powerful Alvis ever sold. Dunn was given carte blanche by John Parkes and he installed a third SU carburettor; the compression ratio went up to 9:1 and larger valves were fitted. This increased power to 150bhp, and one special version put out 154bhp. According to factory figures on the standard model, top speed was now 120mph (118mph with Borg-Warner automatic transmission) and 0–60mph was reached in 9.9sec compared with 11.7sec in the TE 21.

Dunn's father, William, who had played such a large part in the Fourteen and other Alvis cars, had what his son called a 'justifiable preoccupation' with engine power being a minimum of 10 horsepower per litre at 1,000rpm, so that low-speed pulling power was satisfactory. In the TF Mike Dunn achieved 31.9bhp, or more than 10.6bhp per litre, of which he said his father would have been proud. The strength of Chris Kingham's original engine design some 16 years previously had been demonstrated by a near doubling of output. The engine was once revved to 7,200rpm in a sprint, without damage.

Other mechanical changes included water-heated inlet manifolds, a new type of air filter housing, the fitting of a different ZF gearbox, the five-speed S 5-20 instead of the S 5-17 in the TD Series II and TE, and the lightening of clutch operation. Variable-rate springs improved the rear suspension. Cooling was by a thermostatically-controlled Kenlowe fan and the handbrake was made self-adjusting.

Inside, the often-criticized instrument panel in the centre of the car was made smaller and put in front of the driver. There was a bigger heater and an electrically-heated rear window. Two of the coupes were made with power hoods. Prices went up again, the manual saloon now being £3,325 and the coupe £3,433; automatic transmission added another £115 to both. The list of extras included not only power-steering, but also chrome wire wheels, Reutter seats and two-tone paint. There was also the option of a single colour to the owner's choice and what was called 'non-standard' leather seats.

Alvis appeared at the Earls Court motor show for the last time in 1966. The TF 21s on stand 148 were about £1,000 dearer than the Jaguar Mark 10 4.2-litre though, of course, they were very different cars in character.

Despite the desirability of these fast, elegant cars to Alvis enthusiasts, they only sold at the rate of about one car per week, possibly because the body style was now some eight years old, though there is some evidence that Alvis deferred production of the last few to enable them to take part in the ballot for space for their final appearance at Earls Court.

The body was now costing Alvis a third of the retail price of the car, and there were several disputes with Rolls-Royce, Park Ward's owner, about charges. In April 1966, Park Ward announced that due to delays in Alvis chassis deliveries to their Willesden works, and because of other commitments, they would stop Alvis body production in August of that year. By that time they would have delivered 85 out of the last 100 TF bodies. The remaining 15 they would deliver 'in white', that is, uncompleted and untrimmed.

Alvis planned for the cars to be finished by Harold Radford, the Hammersmith coachbuilder, who would be charging £580 per body.

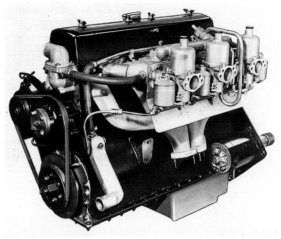

The TF, or Series IV engine; note the water pipe from the thermostat housing leading to the heated inlet manifold. Above right, the three SU carburettors, which with other improvements gave 150bhp and a top speed of 120mph.

Parkes thought this worthwhile as it would enable stocks to be liquidated, even though it would put up the retail price of the car. However, this work was eventually transferred back to Park Ward, who charged an extra £350 per car.

In June 1966, the Alvis board decided to scrap the body tooling for the cars, although production of the final 50 continued. The Alvis service depot at The Hyde, in North London, which had been shared with Armstrong Siddeley, was closed and spares and servicing moved to Henlys in Camden Town. The final TF chassis, number 27475, was completed in the winter of 1966/7; the last three chassis went to Graber in Switzerland and were delivered between October 1966 and February 1967.

However, cars were still being assembled at Park Ward, and in May 1967 the final 15 were ready to be delivered. On August 20, 1967, the last production car, number 27472, was completed at Coventry. The dark blue automatic saloon was registered FLM 167F, according to an Alvis handout, but it is more likely to have been SLM 167F, which corresponded to the registration numbers of that year. It was despatched to Henlys in London, bringing to an end nearly half a century of Alvis car production at Holyhead Road.

Under Rover, old projects such as fighting vehicles were to continue, and new projects, such as gas turbine work and the manufacture of the V8 engine, were soon to begin.

19

WHAT MIGHT HAVE BEEN ...

It was undoubtedly the case that Rover, the new owner of Alvis, wanted to keep the red triangle on the front of a Coventry car. A B Smith, the general manager of Rover and a director of Alvis, was quoted in April 1967 as saying: 'There is no question of giving up the great Alvis name in the range of quality cars. While the present batch production (of the TF) is being run down, consideration is being given to a replacement worthy of the Alvis tradition – but no plans have been finalized for either a prototype or production.'

Some speculative work had been done on a TG 21, which had a TF body and chassis, and a 3-litre engine equipped with six SU carburettors, which produced 206bhp, and this car topped 130mph at the MIRA track. However, the engine would barely run below 3,000rpm and when it once stalled at traffic lights the only way the mechanics could restart it was by putting their arms across the air intakes. There was also an exercise on a new body for what was to be the TA 30, and an underbody was built for test purposes as this was to be the first chassis-less Alvis car.

A design study had been done on a V8/front-wheel-drive arrangement like the Oldsmobile Toronado's, but the preferred arrangement was for rear-wheel drive with a 3.5-litre overhead-cam straight 'six', with studs bolted straight through the block, as in the Rover K-series engines of the Nineties, connecting the cylinder head to the main bearing caps.

There had also been a bizarre proposal from a Mr I J Westwood-Booth, of Hackensack, New Jersey, to manufacture in the United States replica prewar Speed 20s, using American engines. He planned to build 1,000 of these cars in the first year and then 2,400 a year thereafter. Alvis could see no objection as long as the status of Mr Westwood-Booth's syndicate was acceptable and there was a profit in allowing him to use the drawings.

However, the final car project at Holyhead Road was the Rover P6/BS experimental car, although it was built by Alvis and the detailed design and drawing of the running-gear was under Mike Dunn's supervision.

It was first described to the Rover board as a two-seater high-performance sports car 'of unusual design'. There was considered to be a market for 200 cars per week, with some going to North America. The body would come from a specialist manufacturer

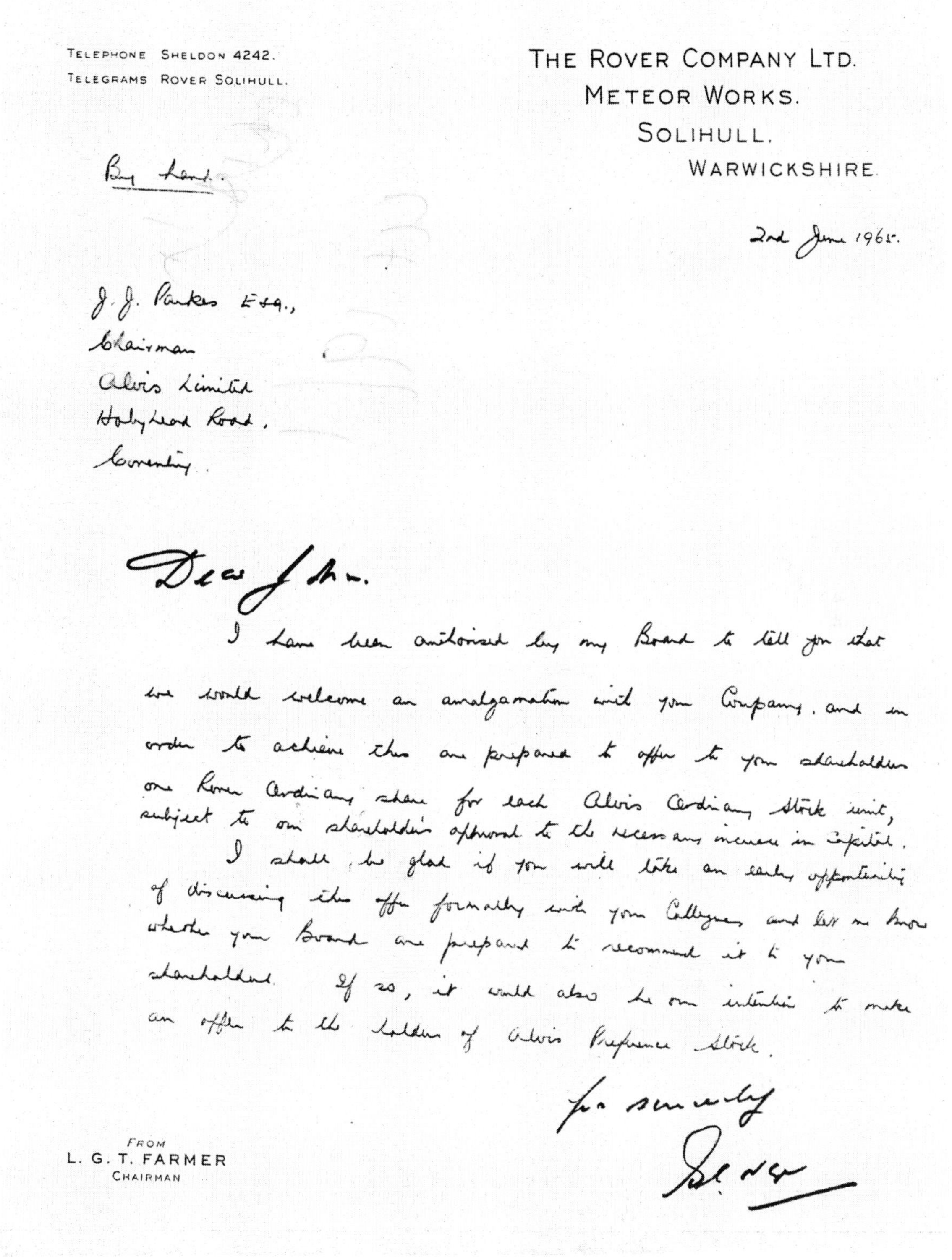

THE ROVER COMPANY LTD.
METEOR WORKS.
SOLIHULL.
WARWICKSHIRE.

2nd June 1965.

By hand.

J. J. Parkes Esq.,
Chairman
Alvis Limited
Holyhead Road,
Coventry.

Dear John,

I have been authorised by my Board to tell you that we would welcome an amalgamation with your Company, and in order to achieve this are prepared to offer to your shareholders one Rover Ordinary share for each Alvis Ordinary stock unit, subject to our shareholders' approval to the necessary increase in capital.

I shall be glad if you will take an early opportunity of discussing this offer formally with your Colleagues and let me know whether your Board are prepared to recommend it to your shareholders. If so, it would also be our intention to make an offer to the holders of Alvis Preference Stock.

Yours sincerely

FROM
L. G. T. FARMER
CHAIRMAN

The letter from Rover to John Parkes suggesting 'amalgamation' with Alvis. In fact, the deed was already well-planned.

such as Abbey Panels, and the original plan was for the car to be built at the Rover works at Solihull. The development cost would be £800,000 and the car would be introduced by June 1970.

Design work had begun at Alvis on January 1, 1966. Spencer King and Gordon Bashford of Rover proposed a mid-engined three-seater sports coupe using the new (to Rover) 3½-litre alloy V8 which was being made under licence from Buick. The interior configuration was unusual in that the third seat was sideways, behind the two front seats.

The engine was slightly tuned to 185bhp and drove forward via a Morse chain into the suitably modified tailshaft of the Rover P6 four-speed gearbox, and from the layshaft to the rear axle unit which was mounted in a special casting that included the engine's sump. The rear hubs were mounted on the ends of a P6-type de Dion tube.

Later proposals than those originally put to the board were for Rover to design and make the body and trim, and Alvis the mechanical parts such as the suspension, steering and driveline. Alvis were set a strict weight target which they managed to beat by a substantial margin, but the body itself was overweight.

Nevertheless, a *Motor* road test of the prototype, which was first driven in early August 1966, talked of superb traction and roadholding, with a top speed of 140mph and tremendous acceleration (0–60mph in 6.6sec). It was to be sold at about £1,500, which was rather more than its similar mid-engined contemporary, the Lotus Europa.

However, in the spring of 1968, Rover fell into the maw of British Leyland and the project was cancelled, then suddenly revived as a matter of urgency a year later, when it was said that several other manufacturers, including BMW and Mercedes, were working on mid-engined sports cars. A final clay model was approved and sent to Pressed Steel for production evaluation, but then the project was suddenly cancelled for the last time. It is said that Sir William Lyons had objected that the BS would compete within the BL empire with his Jaguar E-type. *The Motor* test of the prototype had described it as being uncannily like the Jaguar; others, perhaps more partisan, would have described it as being better!

The car exists still, in the collection of the British Motor Industry Heritage Trust. It is of wry satisfaction to Mike Dunn that if you look underneath, the name ALVIS appears on many of the castings.

The Leyland period at Alvis was not a happy one; those who were there at the time spoke of the difference between the Alvis spirit and philosophy and the corporate sprawl of BL.

There was a further small involvement in the automotive business when Alvis dabbled in what were referred to as 'discreetly-protected vehicles', using their experience in building fighting machinery. Jack Hedges, who replaced Mike Dunn as chief engineer, described them memorably to me as, 'vehicles armoured for the protection of heads of state and the like for use on those occasions when they might reasonably expect to be shot at'.

The publicity said that Alvis would modify any make of large upmarket car, such as Jaguars, Daimlers and Range Rovers, 'because not only do these cars possess the refinements and accommodation befitting a VIP, but with their superior technical specification they

Armoured protection for the rich and famous. A bullet-proof rear end for a Rolls-Royce Phantom.

have sufficient power and strength to cope with the additional weight of armour'. Whether the armour was ever put to the ultimate test is not known.

In July 1981, Leyland sold off Alvis to United Scientific Holdings Ltd for £27 million, and production of military vehicles continued at Holyhead Road until 1991, when the factory was demolished and the 38-acre site cleared for development. Wild tales appeared about a huge cache of parts being discovered and two prewar cars being found entombed. In fact, nothing was ever found, and similarly fanciful tales attended the demolition of the Standard-Triumph factory nearby some months later.

In December 1991, USH, now in a new factory at Walsgrave, in Coventry, with nearly 900 employees, decided to retitle the group Alvis plc, so the name lives on, as does the tradition of engineering in military vehicles, aerospace and transmissions. At the last open day in the works at Holyhead Road in 1989, as Alvis owners and the families of the staff trooped around the shops to see the machinery and what it produced, one Alvis employee showed great pride in being able to manufacture wingflap gearboxes for Boeing and Airbus with a built-in backlash of 4 thousandths of an inch, designed to operate tens of thousands of times with perfect safety. This was an engineering achievement of which T G John, Smith-Clarke and Parkes would have been proud.

Despite John's vision of cars continuing to be the main business of Alvis after the war, the work which was done between 1939 and 1945 changed the nature of the company and made it a defence contractor. There were orders and investment for such work; cars took a much lower priority and consequently, compared with prewar years, the model range was extremely limited. Mistakes were also made.

THE ALVIS STORY

1 LEONIDES MAJOR HELICOPTER ENGINE   2 LEONIDES AERO ENGINE
3 FIRST ALVIS CAR   4 ROVER V8 ENGINE
5 ROVER GAS TURBINE ENGINE   6 ALVIS 3 LITRE COUPE
7 SAMARITAN 8 STRIKER 9 SULTAN 10 SCORPION
11 STALWART 12 SALADIN 13 SALAMANDER 14 SARACEN

The reliance on outside bodybuilders was a source of endless trouble from 1946 until the end of production and made Alvis vulnerable to other people's problems. In addition, there were mistaken ventures like the Willowbrook contract. Projects such as the aborted Three-litre prototype of 1948 and the Issigonis V8 foundered because the company was caught between not being big enough to afford tooling for pressed-steel construction, and not being small enough, like Bristol or Aston Martin, to build a few very expensive cars with bespoke bodies, though the later Park Ward days approached this position.

It is fruitless to speculate upon what might have happened if the deal with Aston Martin had gone through in the Sixties since Sir David Brown has said that he really does not know what he would have done with Alvis. Had the car-making side continued in some form, it might have been swallowed up by one of the American giants in the Eighties, as were Jaguar, Lotus and Aston Martin itself.

Credit is due to John Parkes for keeping car production going as long as he did. During its last 19 years the car division failed to make a profit and sometimes incurred heavy losses, though there is some evidence that it was used to absorb overheads from other areas. Also, it was kept going for the prestige which the cars gave to the Alvis name, a prestige of which those who drive behind the red triangle are still very proud.

By the mid-Sixties car-making was only a small part of the Alvis business.

20

STAYING ON
THE ROAD

Many of the postwar Alvises have now completed a quarter of a million miles and more, and some without the cylinder head being removed. The well-built engines and sturdy chassis have ensured that large numbers have survived the ravages of time and weather. Their status as 'classic' cars has meant that many which might have decayed by the wayside have been rescued and lovingly restored.

However, care is needed in choosing even a restored car. During the classic car price boom in the Eighties, many mouldering wrecks of all makes were dragged out of hedges, patched up by someone handy with a MIG welder and sent on their expensive and uncertain way. The Alvis, particularly the Park Ward variety, needs careful treatment. The golden rule in buying a restored car should always be to ask: 'Who did it, and can I see the bills?'

Even the stout chassis does not guarantee Forth Bridge-type reliability, for box-section chassis can and do hold rainwater trapped in the frame, usually at the lowest point. A particular problem in Three-litre cars is in the area of the rear spring hangers, which tend to be attacked from within and without and may eventually deform and crumble. In my own car they had reached such a stage of advanced decomposition that the rear ends of the leaf springs were carried by enormous shackles knocked up by some blacksmith, who had then drilled and bushed the chassis itself to carry the load. Fortunately, repair sections for the rear are now available. Other parts of the chassis can be plated, but for the really desperate case, a replacement chassis may be needed.

As far as panels are concerned, the rear wings can be troublesome. On the TA/TC cars the rear wheelarch is constructed of aluminium at the front and wood at the rear. The aluminium can set up catalytic corrosion with the bolted-on steel wings, and the wooden section tends to absorb water, which then rusts the adjoining steel. Park Ward cars suffer from rusting in the rear arch where it is double-skinned and spot-welded.

On the TA/TC cars, the point above the B-post can rust along the rain channel, but a more pressing, lurking problem can be corrosion in the metal drainpipes at the four corners of the sunroof housing and the perishing of the rubber hoses which drain the water through the structure of the car. Also, rust flakes and rubbish accumulate in the piping, blocking the egress of water. Since much of the pipework is concealed above the headlining, damp and

discoloration should be attended to quickly as the water will eventually destroy the fabric. In all models water can leak through window seals, causing corrosion in rear sections.

TE/TF nose sections await the rotters at Red Triangle.

The door posts on early Park Ward cars, which caused such trouble, were eventually laminated in the later models, but can still cause problems due to water ingress, and may need bracing if doors do not fit. This can be a job entailing the removal of the front wings, which themselves rot around the headlamp housing. Like most cars, the sill structure can be vulnerable.

Mechanically, apart from the effects of age on moving parts, the cars have few weak points of consequence other than persistent overheating, due to sludging-up of blocks and radiators. There are some who advocate the removal of thermostats and the modification of head gaskets to cure the problem. Brake master cylinders in early Three-litre cars are cast iron and can rust internally, thus dangerously compromising the seal in the cylinder; in my own car, the bottom of the cylinder – after nearly 40 years' use – was badly pitted. The Alvis gearbox in the TA/TC series is robust, but the BMC gearbox in some of the later Park Ward cars was not as satisfactory, and even the ZF replacement can have selector problems.

This is not intended to be a maintenance guide; excellent advice is available from the Alvis Owner Club, which has been in existence more than 40 years, contains experts on all the models of the marque, produces an interesting magazine and organizes functions throughout the year. It has sections thoughout Britain and in North

America, Denmark, Sweden and the Netherlands, and there are enthusiastic club members and owners in many other parts of the world, particularly Australia and New Zealand.

Keeping the cars on the road with spares and repairs since Alvis stopped car production in 1967 has often been with the help of Red Triangle Ltd, of Kenilworth in Warwickshire. British Leyland first offered the entire stock of Alvis spares to Henlys in Coventry, but when this approach failed the Alvis service manager, David Michie, took them over with other Alvis personnel, including Rowland Simmons, who now runs Red Triangle.

The firm's stores in Common Lane are packed with thousands of Alvis parts, some of which are still in their original wrappings. Of the 8,000 lines which Red Triangle sell, many are more than 40 years old, such as the timing wheels for the TA 14. Items like crankshaft pulleys, cylinder heads and flywheels are factory stock, but many engine parts are now remanufactured, such as oil pump gears and bearings and other mechanical parts like wire wheel hubs, kingpins and leaf springs. Every panel for the Park Ward cars is available, including the complicated nose section for the TE/TF, a hand-rolled double-curved item. Timber sections such as A-posts are also available and there are growing stocks of remade parts for the earlier postwar cars.

Simmons, an enthusiast who rallies a Willowbrook TC 108G, is also strong on the restoration side as the firm rebuilds cars from scratch, including upholstery and trim. It is now possible to build a Park Ward car almost as it left the factory, since Three-litre chassis

Restoration cases gradually becoming pristine cars again.

Even the most
discouraging prospect ...

... gradually starts
becoming worthwhile ...

... especially when it leaves the paint shop.

are now being constructed and the five-speed Getrag gearbox, as used in BMWs, has been adapted to suit Alvis engines, as parts for the ZF gearbox are now scarce.

Another firm specializing in Alvis mechanical repairs and body restoration, including ash frame repairs and panel-making, are Bryn Engineering, in Penpergwm, Abergavenny, Gwent. They have been working on Alvis cars for 23 years; Nick Simpson, who runs it, is technical editor of the Alvis Owner Club journal and an acknowledged expert on the marque. Other firms are: SV Restorations, of Billingborough, Sleaford, Lincolnshire, and Chingford Autos, in London E17.

There are also many specialist firms who will make wings and other panels to order. In addition, autojumbles are useful for proprietary parts such as electrical items, and the Alvis Owner Club magazine and the Club's occasional autojumbles are particularly useful for more obscure parts.

The help, advice and spares which are available will keep the red triangle on roads in Britain and throughout the world for very many years to come.

A
Technical
Specifications

Fourteen (TA 14)

Introduced UK: November 1946

Body style: Four-door saloon by Mulliners of Birmingham; two-door drophead coupes by Tickford of Newport Pagnell and Carbodies of Coventry. Many drophead variants and estates by small coachbuilders

Engine: Four-cylinder ohv; RAC rating 13.58hp
Capacity: 1,892cc
Bore: 74mm (1.87in)
Stroke: 110mm (2.79in)
Compression ratio: 6.9:1
Carburation: Single SU H4
BHP (net): 65 at 4,000rpm
Max torque: 95lb.ft at 3,000rpm

Transmission
Clutch: 8 7/8in Borg and Beck A6-G
Gearbox: Alvis four-speed, synchromesh on top three
Overall ratios: 14.46, 9.42, 6.48, 4.875:1
Rear axle ratio: 4.875:1

Suspension: Semi-elliptic leaf springs front and rear with Armstrong double-acting hydraulic dampers

Steering: Marles type 461 cam-and-roller

Brakes: Girling two-leading-shoe, 12in (30.48mm) diameter drums

Wheels: Five-stud Dunlop disc with 6.00 x 6in tyres

Dimensions
Wheelbase: 9ft (274.3cm)
Front track: 4ft 6in (137.1cm)
Rear track: as above
Length: 14ft 7in (444.5cm) – saloon
Width: 5ft 8in (172.7cm)
Height: 5ft 1in (154.9cm)
Ground clearance: 6½in (16.5cm)
Kerb weight: 28cwt (3,136lb/1,423kg)

UK retail price when new: £1,093

TB 14 Sports Tourer

Introduced UK: 1949

As TA 14 except:

Body style: Two-door sports coupe by AP Metalcraft, Coventry

Engine
Carburation: Two SU H4
BHP (net): 68 at 4,000rpm

Transmission
Overall ratios: 12.86, 8.36, 5.76, 4.33:1
Rear axle ratio: 4.3:1

Dimensions
Length: 14ft 6in (441.96cm)
Width: 5ft 6in (167.6cm)
Height: 5ft 1in (154.94cm)
Ground clearance: 6½in (16.5cm)
Kerb weight: 29¾cwt (2,772lb/1,260kg)

UK retail price when new: £1,275

Three-litre (TA 21)

Introduced UK: September 1950

Body style: Four-door saloon by Mulliners of Birmingham; two-door drophead coupe by Tickford of Newport Pagnell

Engine: Six-cylinder ohv
Capacity: 2,993cc (182.6cu in)
Bore: 84mm (3.31in)
Stroke: 90mm (3.54in)
Compression ratio: 6.9:1
Carburation: Solex AAP dual-downdraught (two SU H4 from Nov 1951)
BHP (net): 86 at 3,800rpm (Solex); 93 at 4,000rpm (SU)
Max torque: 147lb.ft at 2,000rpm

Transmission
Clutch: Single-plate Borg and Beck 10in
Gearbox: Alvis four-speed
Overall ratios: 12.68, 8.24, 5.68, 4.27:1
Rear axle ratio: 4.09:1 hypoid-bevel

Suspension: Independent front coil-and-wishbone with Girling telescopic dampers and anti-rollbar; rear semi-elliptic with dampers

Steering: Burman Douglas worm-and-nut

Brakes: Lockheed hydraulic two-leading-shoe in 11in drums

Wheels: Bolt-on disc with 6.40 x 15in tyres

Dimensions
Wheelbase: 9ft 3½in (283.2cm)
Front track: 4ft 6⅝in (183.7cm)
Rear track: 4ft 6⅛in (137.4cm)
Length: 15ft 4½in (468.6cm)
Width: 5ft 6in (167.6cm)
Height: 5ft 3in (160cm)

Ground clearance: 7½in (19cm)
Kerb weight: 28½cwt (3,192lb/1,450kg)

UK retail price when new: £1,597

TB 21

Introduced UK: October 1950

As TA 21 except:

Body style: Two-door sports tourer by AP Panelcraft of Coventry

Engine
Compression ratio: 7:1
Carburation: Single SU H6
BHP (net): 95 at 4,000rpm

Transmission
Gearbox: Alvis four-speed
Overall ratios: 12.15, 7.89, 5.44, 4.09:1

UK retail price when new: £1,597

TC 21/100

Introduced UK: Spring 1953 (TC21), autumn 1953 (TC 21/100)

As TA 21 except:

Engine
Compression ratio: 8:1 in TC 21/100 and many TC 21, though some 7:1
BHP (net): 100 at 4,000rpm, 90 in some TC 21
Max torque: 163lb.ft at 2,000rpm

Transmission
Gearbox: Alvis four-speed
Overall ratios: 11.19, 7.28, 5.01, 3.77:1
Rear axle ratio: 3.77:1 hypoid-bevel

Suspension: Independent front coil-and-wishbone with Girling telescopic dampers and anti-rollbar; rear semi-elliptic with dampers

Steering: Burman Douglas recirculating-ball

Wheels: Bolt-on disc with 6.00 x 15in tyres (TC 21), centre-lock wire wheels (TC21/100)

UK retail price when new: £1,771 (TC 21 saloon), £1,878 (coupe), £1,821 (TC 21/100 saloon)

TD 21 (Series I) (TC 108G data similar)

Introduced UK: TC 108G October 1956, TD 21 October 1958

Body style: Two-door saloon and coupe styled by Graber of Switzerland and built by Willowbrook of Loughborough (TC 108G) and Park Ward of London (TD 21)

Engine: Six-cylinder ohv
Capacity: 2,993cc (182.6cu in)
Bore: 84mm (3.31in)

Stroke: 90mm (3.54in)
Compression ratio: 8:1
Carburation: Two SU H4
BHP (net): 104 at 4,000rpm
Max torque: 152.3lb.ft at 2,500rpm

Transmission
Clutch: Single-plate Borg and Beck 10in
Gearbox: BMC four-speed manual BN4 and BN7; Borg-Warner automatic three-speed. Alvis four-speed TC108G
Overall ratios: (BN4) 11.57, 7.2, 5.01, 3.77:1; (BN7) 11.04, 7.74, 4.93, 3.77:1
Rear axle ratio: 3.77:1 hypoid-bevel

Suspension: Independent front coil-and-wishbone with Girling telescopic dampers and anti-rollbar; rear semi-elliptic with dampers

Steering: Burman Douglas recirculating-ball

Brakes: Lockheed hydraulic two-leading-shoe in 11in drums; front discs optional

Wheels: Bolt-on disc with 6.00 x 15in tyres, or knock-on wire

Dimensions
Wheelbase: 9ft 3½in (283.2cm)
Front track: 4ft 7⅝in (141cm)
Rear track: 4ft 6⅛in (137.4cm)
Length: 15ft 8½in (478.8cm)
Width: 5ft 6in (167.6cm)
Height: saloon 5ft (152.4cm), coupe 4ft 11in (149.9cm)
Ground clearance: 7in (17.8cm)
Kerb weight: 29cwt (3,248lb/1,476kg)

UK retail price when new: TC 108G £3,450, TD 21 £2,993 saloon, £3,293 coupe; Borg-Warner automatic gearbox £134 extra

TD 21 (Series II)

Introduced UK: April 1962; some modifications from March 1959

As Series I except:

Engine
Compression ratio: 8.5:1
Carburation: Two SU H6
BHP (net): 120 at 4,000rpm

Transmission
Gearbox: ZF five-speed from October 1962
Overall ratios (manual): 11.38, 6.97, 4.86, 3.77, 3.07:1

Brakes: Dunlop disc 11½in front, 11in rear

UK retail price when new: £2,882 saloon, £3,157 coupe

TE 21 (Series III)

Introduced UK: October 1963

As TD Series II except:

Engine
Compression ratio: 8.5:1
BHP (net): 130 at 5,000rpm
Max torque: 165lb.ft at 3,250rpm

Transmission
Clutch: Single-plate Borg and Beck DS 10in
Gearbox: ZF all-synchromesh five-speed manual; Borg-Warner automatic three-speed
Overall ratios: manual 11.38, 6.97, 4.86, 3.77, 3.07:1 Automatic 8.17, 5.08, 3.54:1

Suspension: Woodhead Monroe shock aborbers

Steering: Alvis/ZF power-steering optional from October 1964

UK price when new: £2,774 saloon, £3,015 coupe

TF 21 (Series IV)

Introduced UK: March 1966, production ceased August 1967

As TE 21 except:

Engine
Compression ratio: 9:1
Carburation: Three SU HD6
BHP (net): 150 at 4,750rpm
Maximum torque: 185lb.ft at 3,750rpm

Transmission
Gearbox: ZF five-speed manual
Overall ratios: 11.31, 6.43, 4.67, 3.77, 3.21:1

UK retail price when new: £3,225 saloon, £3,433 coupe; automatic £115 extra

B

Performance Figures

This data is extracted from factory figures and contemporary road tests. Since no rigorous road-testing as we now know it was done on the TA 14 and the early TA 21, due to fuel restrictions and other considerations, approximations can be found in the relevant chapters. The TC 21/100 figures are from *The Motor*, the TD and TE from a combination of *The Autocar* and Alvis, and the TF statistics are from the factory tests. They can, of course, vary quite widely; for instance, those who tested the TE 21 for the factory regularly achieved fuel consumption figures in the twenties, although a magazine test recorded much less. Therefore, the figures should be regarded only as indications of performance. All figures are for manual cars; obviously, the Borg-Warner automatic was slower, though not by much in the TF, where top speed was only 2mph less at 118mph. But typically in the TD 21 Series II automatic, the 0–60mph figure was 3 seconds slower, as it was from 0–90mph.

	TC 21/100	TD 21 (SII)	TE	TF
Acceleration (mph/sec)				
0–30	5.3	4.5	4.0	3.8
0–40	7.6	7.2	5.7	5.7
0–50	10.8	9.8	8.5	7.5
0–60	15.4	13.9	11.7	9.9
0–70	20.2	18.4	15.9	13.6
0–80	28.6	24.3	21.0	17.2
0–90	40.6	33.3	30.1	23.5
0–100			45.5	31.5
Maximum speed in gears				
5th			108	120
4th	101.1	102.8	105	111.5
3rd	84	83	81	89.8
2nd	58	58	60	65.2
1st	34	39	36	37.2
Overall fuel consumption (mpg)				
	20.6	17.1	15.9	n/a

C
Production Figures

The Alvis car numbering system is logical because after the war chassis and engine numbers were made to coincide, although body numbers vary between different builders.

However, despite the continuing excellent work done by the Alvis Owner Club in research and production of registers, there are still areas of uncertainty, created by the overlap of numbers between different models and, in some cases, the omission of numbers in a sequence.

In addition, some prototypes were given special numbers, eg 3L1, but others, such as the first Park Ward prototype, were included in the general numbering sequence. Further, the engines sold to Healey bore Alvis numbers which were not used in the chassis sequence. The range of engine/chassis numbers for each model does not, therefore, necessarily coincide with the actual number produced. More details of the breakdown into different body types can be found in the text.

Model	Engine/Chassis numbers	Total
TA 14	20500–23499	
	23600–23802	
	23821–23830	3,210
TB 14	23500–23599	100
TA 21	23803–23820	
	23831–25119	
	25323–25331	1,313
TB 21	25120–25150	31
TC 21	25151–25300	257
TC 21/100	25385–25908	468
TC 108G	25909–25945 (except 25938)	36
TD 21 (I)	25938; 25946–26729	784
TD 21 (II)	26730–27015	285
TE 21 (III)	27016–27367	349
TF 21 (IV)	27370–27475	105
	Total postwar production	6,938